Distress of Souls

To Jean

God Bless

Joseph Dulmage

Distress of Souls

YET TROUBLE CAME

Joseph Dulmage

ISBN-13: 9781530576937
ISBN-10: 1530576938
Library of Congress Control Number: 2016904579
CreateSpace Independent Publishing Platform
North Charleston, South Carolina

Dedicated to my oldest daughter, Heather, afflicted with an extremely rare neuromuscular disease when she was ten years old, she has endured untold physical and psychological anguish for more than thirty years. And to my mother-in-law, Darlene, struggling with Alzheimer's Disease for the last five years. And to my wife, Sue, who takes care of us all.

Weight of Glory

§

2 Corinthians 4:17 For our light affliction,
which is but for a moment, worketh for us a far
more exceeding and eternal weight of glory;

Christian ear I beg thy hearing to ease my dreadful burden.
Perhaps another debtor's view will open wide my curtain?

An awful torment haunts my living, a terror to behold.
If charity commends thee, then hear my tale need told.

Years ago this journey started, my life seemed so complete.
My soul pristine and ever joyous, I sang among the wheat.

Yet down the path I heard the hum, faint- but easily ignored.
I turned away from this distraction, ambitious plans restored.

I barely touched the faithless world as I dined at Caesar's table.
Nothing more than business, just did what kept me stable.

But then the sound grew louder, incessant and profane.
Disrupting dreams and waking hours, I prayed it to restrain.

No dream nor vision do I see, but constant sounds I hear.
Prayer nor sleep dims the noise which perpetrates my fear.

I face myself without the lies, conscience needs to purge.
Then, rather like a memory, awareness doth emerge.

Growth is always measured by the grief of God one feels.
Righteousness cannot be feigned nor virtue can one steal.

I hear the sound of spitting, of mocking, and disdain.
I hear the sound of holiness, I hear the sound of pain.

Murmurings from hidden mouths devoid of very breath.
Expressing moods of evil joy, like devils causing death.

Who they are or why they sing I fear to understand.
Suddenly a voice breaks forth- a trumpet in the band.

He said *I am the Son of God*. Thus we demand the law.
He said we work iniquity, our righteousness is flawed.

Crucify him and we shall see if he saves us and himself.
There's nothing we can't do if God lives only on our shelf.

One voice within the awful noise sounds strangely out of rhyme.
Incongruous, but with the mob, a voice that sounds like mine.

My flesh though reckoned dead, with Holy Spirit clashes.
Wherefore I abhor *myself*, and repent in dust and ashes.

Beholden to faith's constant war, which darkens my life's story
Light afflictions work for me an eternal weight of glory

end

Preface

§

Psalms 34:19 Many are the afflictions of the righteous:
but the LORD delivereth him out of them all.

THIS BOOK OBSERVES SUFFERING FROM a biblical perspective. If a maximum amount of suffering exists, no doubt persons are struggling through it. May God grant them mercy and relief. Christians face two kinds of afflictions in life. The environmental including all griefs out of our control, and afflictions which Christians bring upon themselves through disobedience.

Environmental sufferings comprise geographic locations, oppressive governments, religions, cultures, economies, draughts and hurricanes. The environment also includes birth defects, disease, aging, war, poverty, and birth status. Individual Christians retain little control over such things other than to endure them the best they can.

Self-caused afflictions require a broad latitude of understanding. Curiously, bad choices interact with the environment making personal responsibility hard to define. For instance, an alcoholic endures afflictions due to his own sin, while the same alcoholic's family's suffering is environmental. Similarly, a bad marriage might be explained with the same math. The extent personal sin hurts innocent people is staggering. Dare we consider sins of nations, readers need only use their imaginations to ponder the horrors of human culpability.

Whatever our afflictions and whatever the cause, scripture declares the Lord delivers us *out of them all*. Weighed against *an eternal weight of glory*, afflictions become lighter. Hence the question needs be asked, what is an *eternal weight of glory?*

The same glorious salvation Jesus Christ offers to any lost sinner who believes-also delivers Christians out of all afflictions. Yet, for some Christians, deliverance may not come until heaven. This may seem altogether a failure to explain anything, but consider this:

Afflictions produce sorrow, anguish, frustration, and sometimes anger. But through it all, God weighs heavily on our hearts and minds; one way or another we engage with God. In sadness and despair, Jesus Christ remains the overwhelming truth in a Christian's life. Every trial, pain; and infirmity, every disappointment and heart break- all things develop our relationship with Jesus Christ. God's wondrous promises exist no matter our temporary personal circumstance. This is a great weight, a tremendous spiritual force. When reconciled through prayer, it lifts despairing souls from misery to hope. As we live Jesus Christ is being formed in us. Stepping onto heaven's shore, we will be like him. These glorious truths work for us an eternal weight of glory.

Table of Contents

Part One
Distress of Souls

Observations on Depression, Pain and Sorrow

Psalms 31:9 *Have mercy upon me, O LORD,*
for I am in trouble: mine eye is consumed
with grief, yea, my soul and my belly.

Right Questions: Wrong Answers

§

Romans 8:22 *For we know that the whole creation groaneth and travaileth in pain together until now.*

THE BIBLE DECLARES GOD'S WHOLE creation is in pain: The animal kingdom, plants and forests, oceans and life therein, atmospheric conditions, and human beings are suffering. The Christian theologian traces pain to original sin, the fall of Adam and Eve in the Garden of Eden. But there is little comfort in knowing the ultimate beginning of human suffering. Man's Fall alerts human beings to their need of a Saviour; it does not stop pain. Original sin reveals only the cause- it does not answer the why or purpose; therefore it does not help me (all that much) with personal suffering.

Illustration: A man fighting a war in a foreign country gets his leg blown off when a roadside bomb explodes beneath his vehicle. Ten years later as he struggles with daily life, he knows how he lost his leg; but that knowledge does not help him in his daily life.

When people seek a reason for their misery, they acknowledge pain has a spiritual component. Something inside us seems to insist there must be a divine purpose. Suffering is so prevalent for human beings God must accomplish something important with it; thus personal tragedy becomes a two pronged event;

1. The pain itself.
2. Wondering why suffering is even necessary.

People seeking to know a spiritual or moral reason for their pain often feel frustrated, because the answer to their questions seem elusive if not altogether unanswered.

* How could a loving God allow this?
* Why me?
* Life isn't fair.

For those in pain, the questions surrounding *why* are very important. Somehow if they just knew why God allows their suffering, they believe it may help them cope. Personally, if my wife and I knew why our daughter has a terrible neurological disease, it might make us feel better? Whether or not it would make our daughter feel better is yet another question.

Perhaps a moral reason or justification for personal suffering helps us make sense of this cruel world, at least momentarily? Let me admit right up front, I believe quite strongly many of us may not find a satisfying answer this side of heaven; but with equal conviction I believe wrong answers make things worse.

For example, Mr. Smith smoked cigarettes for decades- acquired cancer, suffered terribly, and died. "Well" someone says, "there is the reason. He smoked; therefore it's his own fault." But what about Mr. Thomas who smoked for just as long, yet happily enjoys good health even as he continues to puff away? And to make it all more perplexing, there is Mr. Jones who never smoked a day in his life and dies of lung cancer at age 32. Not to pick on smokers (they are abused enough) I could paint similar scenarios with overeating, drinking, addictions, abusive life styles of all sorts; alas, I will spare the reader.

Clearly, some human behaviors result in pain and suffering. But our simple judgmental answers fall short of total understanding. Life style mistakes do not justify or ease the pain for innocent people whom their behavior affects. Mr. Smith's early death from lung cancer left his wife and children in poverty. And the consequences of the family's economic situation and fatherless children resulted in great misery. So even if Mr. Smith deserved cancer, his family did not. Sometimes human reasoning makes misery seem more unjust and more complicated. Even for people making the original mistakes, like Adam and Eve, it answers only the cause- not the why. In other words, Adam and Eve and Mr. Smith also lived in pain- society simply interprets their pain less worthy of compassion because *they deserve it*. Which in reality only makes society's suffering less painful by relieving them from empathy; it certainly did not make Mr. Smith's misery any less painful.

How could a loving and just God allow this?

Whatever the tragedy: a bad marriage, cancer, war, poverty, loneliness, birth defects, overwhelming stress, etc., the question, "How could a loving God allow this?" is inevitably asked. The question is appropriate. The answer may not be known, but the wrong answers hurt. For example if one concludes a loving God could not allow the tragedy to happen, what does that mean?

1. There is no God.
2. God does not love; he is indifferent to human suffering.
3. God was incapable to stop it.

Although we do not know why God allowed the tragedy to happen, the Bible assures us God exists, God cares, and God is powerful enough to do anything. Even if suffering delivers us to a place where questioning God's motives surround us like a dark cloud, no value or comfort exists in abandoning established truth. Once we eliminate wrong answers, we progress with our understanding of pain. Lots of questions in life are answered by considering and then eliminating wrong possibilities.

When a reporter asked Thomas Edison if he felt like a failure after over 9,000 failed attempts making the electric light bulb, Edison replied "Why would I feel like a failure? And why would I ever give up? I now know definitively over 9,000 ways that an electric light bulb will not work. Success is almost in my grasp." Shortly after, and over 10,000 attempts, Edison invented the light bulb.

In the Edison story we learn some important explanations for suffering even though none of the reasons comforted the sufferer at the time. No doubt 10,000 failed experiments disappointed Edison and caused huge frustration. But when we step back and look at the big picture several positives come into view. Edison's story is very inspiring. It teaches us a great moral principle epitomizing the reward of hard work and determination.

We admire people who simply do not quit, in spite of overwhelming difficulties. Consider the wounded soldier enduring years of physical therapy to walk again, or the woman whose fight with breast cancer inspires a community to build a health clinic. This book could literally fill thousands of pages with human tragedies that resulted in something good for humanity. Admittedly this *good* did not ease the pain for the person suffering, but it teaches great truths about pain. It is a powerful spiritual force inspiring courage and compassion. And if one recognizes this fact, one makes a tiny step forward in understanding pain.

The opening verse in this chapter *Romans 8:22* declared all creation *travaileth in pain*. God's use of the word *travaileth* is descriptively severe -yet hopeful. Throughout the Bible, a consistent metaphor for severe physical suffering is a woman's labor pains. And just as a certainly as her labor precedes the joy of new life- so does nature's travailing forecast a coming age where suffering is no more; indeed it is a beckoning promise for a new heavens and a new earth. So, no matter how much pain you may presently be in, it is a fact your pain will eventually end.

> ***John 16:21*** *A woman when she is in travail hath sorrow, because her hour is come: but as soon as she is delivered of the child, she remembereth no more the anguish, for joy that a man is born into the world.*

> ***Isaiah 65:17*** *For, behold, I create new heavens and a new earth: and the former shall not be remembered, nor come into mind.*

Suffering dramatically affects unbelievers

Millions of people believe human misery is evidence there is no God. To the question, *how could a loving God allow this?* They answer incorrectly with reasoning along the lines of:

"If God exists, he must be good and just. God would never allow the endless suffering and tragedies that fill this world; therefore, there is no God."

Ironically, unbelievers innately believe if God exists he would be kind and good and just. They also believe God would be all powerful, only an omnipotent God could prevent all suffering. Paradoxically they arrive at some dogmatic truths about God (albeit in their hypothetical reasoning). The atheists' hypothesis that pain and suffering are incompatible with a righteous God- fails to comprehend his eternal purpose. In reality, pain is a momentary distraction, not a permanent feature of God's kingdom. Only audacious human pride and despair brings men to a doctrine of denial, which remarkably is nurtured by faith, the religion of atheism.

Look into the heavens on a clear night. Billions of stars surround the minuscule dot of substance called earth. Beyond man's vision another billion galaxies exist. Science has long acknowledged the mathematical order and rhythm of the universe, from our own solar system's orbital preciseness providing day and night, seasons, and years to a quasar's light emanating astronomical energy. And there it all hangs in a night sky upon nothing but the will of God. The stellar glory of the observable universe may not disclose the reasons for pain and suffering, but it certainly declares the existence of God.

Chapter notes:

Psalms 19:1-3 To the chief Musician, A Psalm of David. The heavens declare the glory of God; and the firmament sheweth his handywork. 2 Day unto day uttereth speech, and night unto night sheweth knowledge. 3 There is no speech nor language, where their voice is not heard.

Psalms 34:19 Many are the afflictions of the righteous: but the LORD delivereth him out of them all.

Ecclesiastes 5:8 If thou seest the oppression of the poor, and the violent taking away of justice and righteousness in a province, marvel not at the matter: for one higher than the high regardeth; and there are higher than they.

Offended in Jesus

§

Luke **7:23** *And blessed is he, whosoever
shall not be offended in me.*

CONSIDER JOHN THE BAPTIST. PROPHET Isaiah, in the Old Testament,
predicted John the Baptist 700 years before his birth. John's mission identified Jesus Christ as Messiah to Israel and then Lord and
Saviour of the world. As far as serving God and living a holy exemplary life is concerned, few people compare with John the Baptist.

Matthew **11:11** *Verily I say unto you, Among them that are born
of women there hath not risen a greater than John the Baptist:*

After John fulfilled his mission to completion, and served God his
whole life, Herod threw him into prison. John committed no crime.
His godly preaching angered King Herod and his wife. When John
informed them their marriage was immoral and wrong, Herod's wife
was outraged. (Herod had married his brother's wife). The biblical
account spares readers the exact details, but the royal couple lived a
decadent and sinful life. John was innocent from any wrong doing-
guilty only of peaching God's righteousness. And for that Herod
sentenced him to prison and eventual execution.

Jesus' response to John's imprisonment is disturbing, but
extremely relevant to our study on pain and suffering. Imagine how

John feels. Imagine being in jail for doing the right thing. John, no doubt, feels abandoned, and alone. John suffers, and where is Jesus? Why doesn't Jesus do anything? John served God fearlessly and consistently, yet Jesus does not even come to see him.

As John sits in prison, Jesus becomes more and more famous. John probably remembers his own prophecy: *He must increase, but I must decrease. John 3:30.* That was certainly true. John sends two of his own disciples to Jesus with an alarming question. John wants to know if Jesus is truly the Messiah. John seems to doubt if Jesus is the Christ. Jesus' answer is powerful and extremely thought provoking.

> *Matthew 11:2-6 Now when John had heard in the prison the works of Christ, he sent two of his disciples, 3 And said unto him,* ***Art thou he that should come, or do we look for another? 4*** *Jesus answered and said unto them, Go and shew John again those things which ye do hear and see: 5 The blind receive their sight, and the lame walk, the lepers are cleansed, and the deaf hear, the dead are raised up, and the poor have the gospel preached to them. 6 And* ***blessed is he, whosoever shall not be offended in me.***

Before looking at Jesus' answer, consider John's question: ***Art thou he that should come, or do we look for another?*** John's pain and suffering takes its toll. Is John truly questioning if Jesus is the one; has John's horrible ordeal provoked disbelief, or perhaps the dire circumstances confuse his thinking? Is john angry? What do you think?

Have you ever considered how much Christians have in common with John the Baptist? John never saw Jesus do any miracles; he only heard about them (or read about them). John must believe by faith those miracles happened. Furthermore, Jesus did not even go to see John. Jesus sent John's disciples back with a report on the supernatural healings he was doing.

Centuries earlier, the Bible prophesized a man was coming who would do healing miracles and preach the gospel to the poor.

Prophets proclaimed those signs identify the Messiah, the very signs Jesus did every day. In other words- addressing the question: Is Jesus the Lord? The answer is written in the Bible; and then the scriptures must be believed by faith.

Jesus knew John believed the Bible, and John certainly knew about those specific prophecies. Indeed, Isaiah, the same prophet predicting Jesus, prophesized about John crying in the wilderness. John himself identified Jesus to Israel! But that part of Jesus' answer is only academic compared to what the Lord says next.

And blessed is he, whosoever shall not be offended in me.

That was Jesus' answer to one of the greatest heroes of the faith who ever lived. Have you ever been offended because Jesus does not answer your prayer? Have you ever been offended by something Jesus says? John wants Jesus to come and see him. But Jesus does not come; John is executed in prison without ever seeing Jesus again (till heaven). What if you were in John's predicament? Would you be offended? Would you doubt? Would you still believe no matter your circumstance? Jesus does not always answer the way we expect.

CHAPTER NOTES:

Definition- Offend: to cause (a person or group) to feel hurt, angry, or upset by something said or done: to be unpleasant to (someone or something): to do wrong: to be against what people believe is acceptable or proper.

Psalms 6:3-4 *My soul is also sore vexed: but thou, O LORD, how long? 4 Return, O LORD, deliver my soul: oh save me for thy mercies' sake.*

Psalms 13:1 *To the chief Musician, A Psalm of David. How long wilt thou forget me, O LORD? for ever? how long wilt thou hide thy face from me?*

Habakkuk 1:2 *O LORD, how long shall I cry, and thou wilt not hear! even cry out unto thee of violence, and thou wilt not save!*

Jeremiah 45:3 *Thou didst say, Woe is me now! for the LORD hath added grief to my sorrow; I fainted in my sighing, and I find no rest.*

Isaiah 40:3 *The voice of him that crieth in the wilderness, Prepare ye the way of the LORD, make straight in the desert a highway for our God.*

John 1:23 *He said, I am the voice of one crying in the wilderness, Make straight the way of the Lord, as said the prophet Esaias.*

John 1:32-36 *And John bare record, saying, I saw the Spirit descending from heaven like a dove, and it abode upon him. 33 And I knew him not: but he that sent me to baptize with water, the same said unto me, Upon whom thou shalt see the Spirit descending, and remaining on him, the same is he which baptizeth with the Holy Ghost. 34 And I saw, and bare record that this is the Son of God. 35 Again the next day after John stood, and two of his disciples; 36 And looking upon Jesus as he walked, he saith, Behold the Lamb of God!*

Not My Will

§

> **Romans 8:26-27** *Likewise the Spirit also helpeth our infirmities:* **for we know not what we should pray for as we ought:** *but the Spirit itself maketh intercession for us with groanings which cannot be uttered. 27 And he that searcheth the hearts knoweth what is the mind of the Spirit, because he maketh intercession for the saints according to the will of God.*

HAS LIFE EVER THROWN YOU a curve ball, or perhaps something more like a hand grenade? Have uncontrollable circumstances taken you to a place you don't want to be? Is it possible God allowed something in your life that offended you? If your answer is yes, dear reader, you are not alone.

When something difficult or terrible happens to a Christian; and God seems to ignore his/her prayers, several things Christians' can know for certain. Facts about God that never change.

God definitely hears Christians' prayers. God is omniscient so it's impossible for him not to hear. He also knows your prayers' concern, and he cares. When people say, *God never heard or never answered my prayer.* What they mean is their request or the solution they want has not happened, which is an entirely different matter than God not hearing them. God responds to their situation, regardless of him not responding the way their prayers request.

Even if it looks like God isn't doing anything, the Lord is active in Christians' lives.

Knowing these facts presents Christians with some hard realities and perhaps alternative choices: Change your prayer to include *if it be God's will*. Ask God to reveal what He wants. Admittedly, this can be very hard especially when *our will* sees absolutely no reason why God would disagree with us.

When doctors told my wife and me our 10 year old daughter, Heather, has a rare neurological disease, we immediately prayed to God for healing; but God did not heal Heather. Thirty years later we still pray. Personally, I have actually asked God to forgive me for praying so much over this same issue. I am concerned I've not accepted the will of God. This may seem like an odd confession, but I want the reader to know. But I also believe God hears our prayers, and he is involved with our family. My wife and I do not understand why our daughter suffers, but our trust and hope in God remains secure. Whatever God's purpose for allowing tragedies into the lives of Christians remains in the wisdom of Christ (for now).

There is scriptural precedent for Christians to stubbornly keep praying; Jesus called it importunity. *The definition of importunity is to: press or urge with troublesome persistence; request or beg urgently.* Interestingly, Jesus gives the *importunity parable* immediately after teaching his Apostles the so called *Lord's Prayer*.

IMPORTUNITY PARABLE, LUKE 11:5-9

(Paraphrase) A man receives unexpected visitors in the middle of the night, and he does not have enough food to be hospitable. Due to the late hour, stores are closed; so he goes and bangs on his friend's door and asks to borrow some food. His friend complains it's too late- and for him to go away- But the man will not leave without food. Alas the importunity of the man's request means the only way for the friend to get rid of the man is to give him some food. So finally the man gets the food he wants.

> **Luke 11:5-9** *And he said unto them, Which of you shall have a friend, and shall go unto him at midnight, and say unto him, Friend, lend me three loaves;* **6** *For a friend of mine in his journey is come to me, and I have nothing to set before him?* **7** *And he from within shall answer and say, Trouble me not: the door is now shut, and my children are with me in bed; I cannot rise and give thee.* **8** *I say unto you, Though he will not rise and give him, because he is his friend, yet because of his importunity he will rise and give him as many as he needeth.* **9** *And I say unto you, Ask, and it shall be given you; seek, and ye shall find; knock, and it shall be opened unto you.*

Some teachers believe when Christian's pray and include the words *if it be thy will* they are literally expressing doubt and a lack of faith. This teaching is incorrect and unbiblical. Some prayer requests would be just plain silly not too pray *not my will Lord, but thine be done.* When making career choices, or choosing a church, choosing a college, finding a house to buy, etc. are just a few obvious examples when asking God's will to supersede your own desire is wise. Praying for God's choice in a husband or a wife certainly merits God's wisdom, especially if you have to make a choice between more than one potential spouse. Because being married is no guarantee of not being lonely, nor does marriage ensure one's happiness. Indeed, a bad marriage can be terrible suffering. May God's will be revealed to you in all your important prayers.

Unless we pray for something or someone where scripture declares the will of God in writing (like for lost souls) or whether we should forgive someone- it is never wrong to ask God's will to overrule our own desires. The context of this study, however, is addressing very hard issues; people in great distress, or going through some fiery trial. Imagine praying for an elderly parent who suffers with cancer and appears to be at death's door, could you conclude your prayer with *Lord your will be done*? What if it was your husband or wife? What if it was your own child? I believe it's wise to let God know we humbly seek his will, even if his will conflicts with our will. And, without question, this takes courage and surrender to God.

Much human suffering directly involves physical health issues. This study is not denying God heals people physically today. I am saying, however, the Bible does not promise it. Christians often find themselves, or someone they love, suffering from disease or serious affliction. Some are delivered, some are not. Sometimes those healed become ill again and are not delivered a second time. But even when we desperately want and pray for God to act- we should not pretend the Bible says something it does not.

Remarkably, the most visible part of Jesus' earthly mission was to relieve pain. Everywhere Jesus went he healed the sick, cured the deaf, brought sight to the blind, and cast out devils. Without a doubt this made him tremendously famous. Scripture makes it very clear, the healing miracles identified Jesus as the Messiah, thereby establishing his authority to forgive sins. Jesus' primary purpose was to save a person from their sins, which allows those who believe into heaven. Below, Jesus used a person's physical disease to illustrate this very important point.

> *Matthew 9:2-7 And, behold, they brought to him a man sick of the palsy, lying on a bed: and Jesus seeing their faith said unto the sick of the palsy; Son, be of good cheer; thy sins be forgiven thee. 3 And, behold, certain of the scribes said within themselves, This man blasphemeth. 4 And Jesus knowing their thoughts said, Wherefore think ye evil in your hearts? 5 For whether is easier, to say, Thy sins be forgiven thee; or to say, Arise, and walk? 6 But that ye may know that the Son of man hath power on earth to forgive sins, (then saith he to the sick of the palsy,) Arise, take up*

thy bed, and go unto thine house. *7 And he arose, and departed to his house.*

Observation: this is an informative account on suffering. Notice the man is sick of the palsy. What's the palsy? The palsy is some undefined illness; therefore it represents disease in general. The man is so sick he can't even walk. The illness is killing him. The person with the palsy is a type (or picture) of you. And some day, a disease or affliction is going to kill you too. (Raptured saint's only exception) With that in mind let us examine the text.

Physical health is very important to us, but to God it's the forgiveness of sins that really matters, because forgiveness of sins allows people into heaven. This is very hard doctrine to a person who is in terrible pain with illness or for persons in empathetic agony watching a loved one suffer. Nevertheless it is a salient truth about pain and suffering.

When Jesus asks, *what's easier, forgiving sins or miraculously healing a terminally ill person?* The answer is only God could do either one. Read *Matthew 9:6* carefully. The reason Jesus healed the man was to identify himself as the one who could forgive sins. The healing was secondary. In fact the Lord seems to trivialize the physical pain. Jesus tells the man, *Son, be of good cheer, thy sins be forgiven thee.* Even though the man is sick and in misery, Jesus' already accomplished his primary mission when he forgave the man's sins, because now the man is ready to go to heaven.

But the facts remain, the man is still sick, his friends and family are still anguished and upset when Jesus says to be cheerful! No one felt like being cheerful. It is true the man is about to be healed, but the man (or his friends) did not know that. They hoped Jesus would heal him, and they knew Jesus could heal him. But would he? The man received his physical healing after his sins were forgiven. This is exactly what happens to a Christian. Ultimately, a Christian gets his physical health (redeemed body) in the future.

This window into the way God views our suffering exemplifies a great truth. A believer's grief, no matter how severe is temporary; heaven is forever. Sometimes the only thing we can do is to weigh our pain against an eternal weight of glory. Let's say a person suffers terribly for 70 years, then dies and goes to heaven. 10,000 years later the earthly suffering will be a tiny sliver of distant memory.

But can we hope for a miracle now? Is it possible to be healed today by faith? YES, God heals people today. And health is always worth praying for. God expects us to pray for healing when our loved ones or we experience afflictions. And prayer often moves God to heal, but don't conclude anything negative about God or yourself if the healing does not come. No amount of prayer changes the written words of God. And God has not promised us perfect health while living in our present bodies. If a Christian's prayer moves God to work a miracle-Glory to God! But if a Christian does not get healed it does not mean he/she has little faith, or that God does not love him/her. Why some Christians live with illness and affliction and others do not remains God's business. Tragic situations do not defeat God's will, in fact, they may accomplish things impossible for us to comprehend.

Many situations cannot be understood this side of heaven. Although you may live in great distress, pray God gives you wisdom and strength to trust him. Faith, hope, and charity are powerful weapons in the battle against pain. Through faith and hope, we know God is good, and he promises us an eternity of happiness.

Throughout the ages, God's people lived a life of faith in spite of their circumstances. Occasionally God displayed miracles, but the spectacular miracles were always the exception, not the rule. Faith pleases God. Pain and heartache are nothing new. Believers' endured hardships and suffering for thousands of years. When and where mighty signs and wonders show up is God's business.

Suffering and pain exist within the body of Christ; those who deny it choose fantasy over truth. Unless we are raptured, our future here ends in hospital beds and graveyards. Every healthy day we enjoy on earth is due to God's mercy and his grace. Our health is something we thank God for, it is not something we demand. All creation waits for deliverance from pain.

CHAPTER NOTES

Psalms 65:2 O thou that hearest prayer, unto thee shall all flesh come.

Psalms 147:3-5 He healeth the broken in heart, and bindeth up their wounds. **4** He telleth the number of the stars; he calleth them all by their names. **5** Great is our Lord, and of great power: his understanding is infinite.

John 11:33 When Jesus therefore saw her weeping, and the Jews also weeping which came with her, he groaned in the spirit, and was troubled,

Isaiah 55:8-9 For my thoughts are not your thoughts, neither are your ways my ways, saith the LORD. **9** For as the heavens are higher than the earth, so are my ways higher than your ways, and my thoughts than your thoughts.

Acts 18:21 But bade them farewell, saying, I must by all means keep this feast that cometh in Jerusalem: but I will return again unto you, **if God will.** And he sailed from Ephesus.

Peter 4:19 Wherefore let them that **suffer according to the will of God** commit the keeping of their souls to him in well doing, as unto a faithful Creator.

Isaiah 35:5-6 Then the eyes of the blind shall be opened, and the ears of the deaf shall be unstopped. **6** Then shall the lame man leap *as an hart, and the tongue of the dumb sing: for in the wilderness shall waters break out, and streams in the desert.*

Revelation 21:4 *And God shall wipe away all tears from their eyes; and there shall be no more death, neither sorrow, nor crying, neither shall there be any more pain: for the former things are passed away.*

Isaiah 53:3-4 *He is despised and rejected of men; a man of sorrows, and acquainted with grief: and we hid as it were our faces from him; he was despised, and we esteemed him not.* **4** *Surely he hath borne our griefs, and carried our sorrows: yet we did esteem him stricken, smitten of God, and afflicted.*

Stressed Out Believers

§

IF MISERY LIKES COMPANY:
Several notable believers became so distraught over stress and disappointments in their life, they actually seemed ready to quit, and some wanted to die. Job, Mrs. Job, Moses, Solomon, Elijah, Jeremiah, (to name a few) were frustrated and hurt by what life threw at them. As the reader can see from the passages below- coming to one's wits' end is nothing new:

MOSES

Overburdened with the responsibility of leading Israel in the wilderness, Moses cries out to God, He is exasperated and overcome with pressure. Scripture clearly depicts his frustrations and despair. Moses' situation is worthy of notice. Not only because he's a major prophet, but it shows anyone can be severely depressed even doing the perfect will of God.

> *Numbers 11:14-15 I am not able to bear all this people alone, because it is too heavy for me. 15 And if thou deal thus with me, **kill me, I pray thee, out of hand,** if I have found favour in thy sight; and let me not see my wretchedness.*

KING SOLOMON

The wisest and richest of all kings (and men) greatly disappointed in life, unsatisfied, and unhappy declares hatred for living. In Solomon's case, rebellion and sin definitely played a role in misery, even so his life teaches important lessons. Wealth, genius, good physical health, possessions, unlimited sex, and power do not make one happy. A high IQ does not impress the one who made the human brain. Nor does intelligence and riches make it easier to escape pain and suffering. Observe what the king who has everything says about his own life.

> *Ecclesiastes 2:17 Therefore I hated life; because the work that is wrought under the sun is grievous unto me: for all is vanity and vexation of spirit.*

Believers do well to study King Solomon, especially when considering reasons for sorrow. King Solomon was not a happy man. God used Solomon's life and wisdom to convey important information about pain and suffering, especially depression. Clearly, God works with tragedy and sorrow to accomplish spiritually valuable lessons in believers' lives. Critical shaping of the heart is sculptured in the valley far more than on a mountain top. Who among us desires wisdom and knowledge? Notice it comes with a price. Yet God also instructs us to desire those cognitive and spiritual virtues. A satisfying relationship with God cannot be achieved without sorrow; paradoxically, joy in the Lord depends on it. (King Solomon is featured in the chapter: Backsliding)

> *Ecclesiastes 1:18 For in much wisdom is much grief: and he that increaseth knowledge increaseth sorrow.*

> *Proverbs 3:13-15 Happy is the man that findeth wisdom, and the man that getteth understanding. 14 For the merchandise of it is*

better than the merchandise of silver, and the gain thereof than fine gold. **15** *She is more precious than rubies: and all the things thou canst desire are not to be compared unto her.*

Ecclesiastes 7:3 *Sorrow is better than laughter: for by the sadness of the countenance the heart is made better.*

JONAH

Like King Solomon, rebellion and disobedience played a role in Jonah's despair. Jonah knew exactly what the Lord wanted him to do, but refused and disobeyed. Backsliding and rebellion is nothing new. Nevertheless, Jonah came to a place where disappointment brought him to his knees. Rebellion does indeed cause stress, anguish, depression, and even suicidal thoughts. A tremendous lesson from Jonah is God never abandons his people; even when believers run from him. God stays with Jonah through his darkest days. An often overlooked and agonizing fact is when Jonah asked God to kill him, he was finally obeying the Lord. This perfectly epitomizes a believer being extremely angry with God. Jonah openly declares his disagreement with God's actions.

Jonah 4:1-4 But it displeased Jonah exceedingly, and he was very angry. *2 And he prayed unto the LORD, and said, I pray thee, O LORD, was not this my saying, when I was yet in my country? Therefore I fled before unto Tarshish: for I knew that thou art a gracious God, and merciful, slow to anger, and of great kindness, and repentest thee of the evil. 3 Therefore now, O LORD,* **take, I beseech thee, my life from me; for it is better for me to die than to live.** *4 Then said the LORD, Doest thou well to be angry?*

Thought to ponder: Working as a chaplain in a prison, I have known prisoners come to Christ who committed heinous and extremely disturbing crimes. So heinous, in fact, that other Christians (in church) upon hearing about the prisoners' salvation were actually disappointed or refused to believe the prisoners got saved. The truth is God saves sinners. And some sinners can find forgiveness and mercy from no one but God. This, I think, comes close to the way Jonah felt about the Ninevites.

ABIGAIL

Abigail, trapped in a loveless marriage, and her husband, Nabal, an enemy to the Lord, found herself in a terrible predicament. Political unrest abounded in Israel, the nation itself suffered under tremendous stress. At the time, King Saul persecuted David and his men and pursued them through the wilderness. Not long before David helped Nabal by protecting his property and his livestock.

Desperate and hungry, David asked Nabal for provisions. By refusing to help, the incident revealed Nabal's loyalty to King Saul. Enraged and feeling betrayed, David prepared to destroy the house of Nabal.

Through no fault of her own, Abigail's entire household was about to be destroyed. Just imagine her emotional distress. In spite of all this, Abigail did not fall apart. Although the situation looked helpless, she acted wisely and hoped for God's providence. Facing eminent death, she persevered and did the right thing. God honored Abigail's effort. She saved her household and God blessed her in ways no one could predict. The lesson learned: Serve God the best you can. No one knows the future; deliverance may just be just around the corner.

1 Samuel 25:3 Now the name of the man was Nabal; and the name of his wife Abigail: and she was a woman of good understanding, and of a beautiful countenance: but the man was churlish and evil in his doings; and he was of the house of Caleb

1 Samuel 25:23-32 And when Abigail saw David, she hasted, and lighted off the ass, and fell before David on her face, and bowed herself to the ground, 24 And fell at his feet, and said, Upon me, my lord, upon me let this iniquity be: and let thine handmaid, I pray thee, speak in thine audience, and hear the words of thine handmaid. 25 Let not my lord, I pray thee, regard this man of Belial, even Nabal: for as his name is, so is he; Nabal is his name, and folly is with him: but I thine handmaid saw not the young men of my lord, whom thou didst send. 26 Now therefore, my lord, as the LORD liveth, and as thy soul liveth, seeing the LORD hath withholden thee from coming to shed blood, and from avenging thyself with thine own hand, now let thine enemies, and they that seek evil to my lord, be as Nabal.

27 And now this blessing which thine handmaid hath brought unto my lord, let it even be given unto the young men that follow my lord. 28 I pray thee, forgive the trespass of thine handmaid: for the LORD will certainly make my lord a sure house; because my lord fighteth the battles of the LORD, and evil hath not been found in thee all thy days. 29 Yet a man is risen to pursue thee, and to seek thy soul: but the soul of my lord shall be bound in the bundle of life with the LORD thy God; and the souls of thine enemies, them shall he sling out, as out of the middle of a sling. 30 And it shall come to pass, when the LORD shall have done to my lord according to all the good that he hath spoken concerning thee, and shall have appointed thee ruler over Israel; 31 That this shall be no grief unto thee, nor offence of heart unto my lord, either that thou hast shed blood causeless, or that my lord hath avenged himself: but when the LORD shall have dealt well with my lord, then remember thine handmaid.

32 *And David said to Abigail, Blessed be the LORD God of Israel, which sent thee this day to meet me:.*

NAOMI AND RUTH

Trying to escape famine, an Israeli family migrated to the country of Moab to start a new life. Soon after settling down, the husband died, leaving his wife, Naomi, and two sons alone. Both Naomi's sons married wives from the country of Moab. The women's' names were Orpah and Ruth. After about ten years, tragedy struck again. Both Orpah's and Ruth's husband died. So Naomi, Ruth, and Orpah found themselves widows.

For more than a decade Naomi experienced trauma, anguish, and sorrow. She endured famine, lost a husband, and both her children. Distraught and grieving, Naomi cries out to those around her. Perhaps she views the misfortune as judgment for leaving Israel and living in Moab? Or perhaps she has no idea why such terrible things have befallen her, but she knows God is involved. Before being too critical of Naomi, remember it was probably her husband's idea to leave Israel and seek help in Moab. Many times the decisions of others place innocent persons in harm's way. Whatever the case, Naomi finds herself in trouble.

> **Ruth 1:20-21** *And she said unto them, Call me not Naomi, call me Mara: for the Almighty hath dealt very bitterly with me.* **21** *I went out full, and the LORD hath brought me home again empty: why then call ye me Naomi, seeing the LORD hath testified against me, and the Almighty hath afflicted me?*

Before Naomi returned to Israel she said goodbye to her two daughters-in-law. At this point in the narrative Naomi reaches her lowest moment. Whether Naomi is overcome with grief and anger toward God, or she is simply a long time backslider only God knows. Although her two daughters-in law want to travel with her to Bethlehem, Naomi urges them toward false religion, she actually discourages both Ruth and Orpah from coming to Bethlehem. Orpah went her own way, but Ruth determined to go to Israel.

Ruth's determination won the day. Despite being a widow, (which in those days was very, very hard) childless, poor, and just awakening to the true God- Ruth bravely traveled to a place of hope and trust in God. Ruth and Naomi traveled to Bethlehem.

Once in Israel, life was hard. Ruth worked the fields for wealthy landowners. Being from a foreign country, men considered her a migrant farm worker, and racially inferior. What chance would she have in this strange new place? Although Ruth or Naomi had no plans of their own, God already set them on a path toward restoration, forgiveness, and a fulfilling life. Ruth becomes happily married to a wealthy and respected business man. True evidence of God's providence in all these struggles is Ruth becomes the great grandmother to King David. And Naomi is restored to a place of faith.

Ruth 1:14-16 And they lifted up their voice, and wept again: and Orpah kissed her mother in law; but Ruth clave unto her. 15 And she said, Behold, thy sister in law is gone back unto her people, and unto her gods: return thou after thy sister in law. 16 And Ruth said, Intreat me not to leave thee, or to return from following after thee: for whither thou goest, I will go; and where thou lodgest, I will lodge: thy people shall be my people, and thy God my God:

Ruth 1:22 So Naomi returned, and Ruth the Moabitess, her daughter in law, with her, which returned out of the country of Moab: and they came to Bethlehem in the beginning of barley harvest.

Ruth 4:13-22 So Boaz took Ruth, and she was his wife: and when he went in unto her, the LORD gave her conception, and she bare a son. 14 And the women said unto Naomi, Blessed be the LORD, which hath not left thee this day without a kinsman, that his name may be famous in Israel. 15 And he shall be unto thee a restorer of thy life, and a nourisher of thine old age: for thy daughter in law, which loveth thee, which is better to thee than seven sons, hath born him. 16 And Naomi took the child, and laid it in her bosom, and became nurse unto it. 17 And the women her neighbours gave it a name, saying, There is a son born to Naomi; and they called his name Obed: he is the father of Jesse, the father of David. 18 Now these are the generations of Pharez: Pharez begat Hezron, 19 And Hezron begat Ram, and Ram begat Amminadab, 20 And Amminadab begat Nahshon, and Nahshon begat Salmon, 21 And Salmon begat Boaz, and Boaz begat Obed, 22 And Obed begat Jesse, and Jesse begat David.

PROPHET JEREMIAH

The Prophet Jeremiah lived an anguishing life. For decades, he endured loneliness, and sorrow. Bible students know him as the *weeping prophet*. God denied Jeremiah even the companionship of a wife. He traveled alone, rarely receiving any fellowship or human support.

Jeremiah's strong stand for God brought him great affliction and mockery from the community. Falsely imprisoned, he served time in wretched conditions. Jeremiah lived in an age when God poured out his judgments on the nation of Judah. His country's slow moral decay tortured the righteous prophet. He endured years of horrible war as Babylon invaded and cruelly conquered Israel, culminating with the destruction of the temple and taking the Jews into the captivity. All of this brought Jeremiah into dark and anguishing depression.

Jeremiah 20:14-18 Cursed be the day wherein I was born: let not the day wherein my mother bare me be blessed. 15 Cursed be the man who brought tidings to my father, saying, A man child is born unto thee; making him very glad. 16 And let that man be as *the cities which the LORD overthrew, and repented not: and let him hear the cry in the morning, and the shouting at noontide; **17** Because he slew me not from the womb; or that my mother might have been my grave, and her womb to be always great with me. **18** Wherefore came I forth out of the womb to see labour and sorrow, that my days should be consumed with shame?*

Sin and rebellion directly caused Judah's misery. Sometimes judgment can be explained, but let us never forget even God's righteous judgment afflicts many innocents, from children to men and women caught up in an evil time.

Amos 5:13 *Therefore the prudent shall keep silence in that time; for it is an evil time.*

Ecclesiastes 9:12 *For man also knoweth not his time: as the fishes that are taken in an evil net, and as the birds that are caught in the snare; so are the sons of men snared in an evil time, when it falleth suddenly upon them.*

Although Prophet Jeremiah endures misery, he never forgets hope and mercy win in the end. The ever constant fact that God is good, kind, and merciful remains unforgotten. Likewise, Christians should always acknowledge the eternity of blessing and happiness yet to come. Never forget we live forever in heaven. Remembering heaven prescribes the best medicine for depression and misery. Sing about heaven. Praise the Lord for heaven. Pray for God's Kingdom to come, and tell others about it- no matter how you feel. Over and over again we see suffering believers engage in hoping and believing in the Lord's promises, a glorious eternal weight of glory.

Jeremiah 33:9-11 *And it shall be to me a name of joy, a praise and an honour before all the nations of the earth, which shall hear* *all the good that I do unto them: and they shall fear and tremble for all the goodness and for all the prosperity that I procure unto it. 10 Thus saith the LORD; Again there shall be heard in this place, which ye say shall be desolate without man and without beast, even in the cities of Judah, and in the streets of Jerusalem, that are desolate, without man, and without inhabitant, and without beast, 11 The voice of joy, and the voice of gladness, the voice of the bridegroom, and the voice of the bride, the voice of them that shall say, Praise the LORD of hosts: for the LORD is good; for his mercy endureth for ever: and of them that shall bring the sacrifice of praise into the house of the LORD. For I will cause to return the captivity of the land, as at the first, saith the LORD.*

Prophet Elijah

Elijah's life epitomizes trauma and trouble; the next chapter in this book is dedicated to him. Mighty in deeds and miracles, Elijah lived a life of righteousness, solitude, and sorrow. Elijah, one of only three men in the Old Testament who never died: *Enoch, Melchizedek, Elijah.* God took him alive to heaven in a whirlwind. In the New Testament, Elijah and Moses stood with Jesus on a mountain and witnessed the Lord Jesus' transfiguration. God used Elijah to teach the wayward nation of Israel the dangers of idolatry; he urged the people to return to the one true God. On top of Mount Carmel, he stood alone against 450 Baal prophets and their wicked King Ahab. Elijah prayed for God to send fire down from heaven and consume the sacrifice. Spectacular displays of God's power, and answered prayer filled this prophet's life. Yet exhausted, lonely, and weary of circumstances beyond his control, he wanted to quit and prayed for God to take his life.

1 Kings 19:3-4 And when he saw that, he arose, and went for his life, and came to Beersheba, which belongeth to Judah, and *left his servant there. **4** But he himself went a day's journey into the wilderness, and came and sat down under a juniper tree: and **he requested for himself that he might die; and said, It is enough; now, O LORD, take away my life;** for I am not better than my fathers.*

Letting God know how we feel

As we can see from reading this brief sketch of stressed out saints from the past, suffering takes its toll on the best and strongest believers. Observe the honesty in these saints' prayers. We, likewise, should not keep our complaints or pain bottled up inside; rather bring it to Jesus in prayer. If you feel awful and mistreated – tell God the truth. Go to him in sincere anguish and defeat. Life can get very difficult. You may well be traveling an emotionally and/or physically tortuous road that few others even comprehend. In the best way you can- take your pain to Jesus. Job-Moses-Solomon- Elijah- Jeremiah all got back up and continued the battle. And so will you; it's your choice.

If a person chooses unbelief in God because of tragedy, what does this accomplish? Would it make the anguish go away? Does not believing make the pain less? If a Christian decides to quit serving the Lord, what does this mean? Where is he/she going to go?

After Jesus said some very difficult and hard sayings many people left him. Then the Lord asked his Apostles if they also planned to leave. Apostle Peter's answer is tremendous. He simply asks- where would they go? And then says, *thou hast the words of eternal life.*

No matter your pain, whatever the injustice, Jesus Christ is still Lord. If things are awful for you right now, just remember no meaningful alternative exists apart from God. Remember all suffering ends for the Christian. Personally, I conclude an existence apart from God makes things utterly hopeless, unbelief is not even possible for me. That does not mean I understand everything God

is currently doing, but trusting him for a better future is very relieving; and paradoxically, makes the present circumstances much better. Nothing wrong here that heaven won't fix.

*John 6:67-69 Then said Jesus unto the twelve, Will ye also go
away? 68 Then Simon Peter answered him, Lord, to whom shall
we go? thou hast the words of eternal life. 69 And we believe and
are sure that thou art that Christ, the Son of the living God.*

What Doest Thou Here?

***1 Kings 19:9** And he came thither unto a cave, and lodged there; and, behold, the word of the LORD came to him, and he said unto him, What doest thou here, Elijah?*

No one in the Bible ever got more stressed out or more depressed than Prophet Elijah. Believers who reach their wits end can learn from this Old Testament saint. To be sure your own circumstances are not Elijah's situation, but your emotional and spiritual reality may be very similar? Anyone whose responsibilities become overwhelming and feels completely defeated, Elijah's bio is for you. Stress, failure, success, exhaustion, loneliness, courage, and faith are some of the intense experiences comprising Elijah's high adrenalin life adventures.

Due to years of Israel's disobedience and refusing to repent, the Lord sent judgment on his favored nation. Elijah prayed for the rain to stop and Israel endured a 3 ½ year draught. The people, especially King Ahab and Queen Jezebel blamed Elijah for turning off the water. They sought tirelessly throughout Israel and even other countries looking for him. When they finally caught up with him, Elijah ordered a national confrontation on a mountaintop. *1 Kings chapter 18* records the events. Below is a paraphrase of the chapter.

Elijah presented himself to King Ahab and told him to gather the people, and 450 Baal prophets to the top of Mount Carmel. After more than three years of no rain, the people finally agreed to listen to God's prophet. Elijah ordered 450 false prophets to prove their god's power by calling fire down from heaven. For hours these false prophets prayed and danced, and carried on begging Baal to prove his power with fire. Of course nothing happened because Baal existed only in the minds of the people. Elijah mocked the false prophets and warned the people to repent and return to the true God. He then repaired the Lord's altar and set the sacrifice in order. After soaking the sacrifice and the altar with water, Elijah prayed for God to reveal himself. Instantly, fire from heaven fell consuming not only the sacrifice, but the stone altar, all the water, and even the dirt on which the altar was constructed. Needless to say, this greatly impressed the spectators and many turned their hearts to the God of Israel. Elijah then commanded the 450 Baal prophets to be slain. Once the people obeyed these orders, Elijah prayed for rain. The rains came and the people rejoiced.

A great victory prevailed in Israel that day: God judged and killed 450 evil religious leaders, revival in Israel commenced, and the drought ended. The famine, now subsided and the nation begins to recover. But not everyone rejoiced. When the wicked Queen Jezebel heard about Elijah killing her false prophets, she went into a rage. She sent orders to find and kill Elijah. She vowed all the nation's power and resources to accomplish her commands.

One may think after Elijah's mighty victory on Mount Carmel, he would scoff at Jezebel's threat. Just think about the tremendous miracles Elijah witnessed that day. Consider the power God gave him and the answered prayers. But Elijah actually seemed to have a breakdown. After his courageous and emotionally charged mountain top experience, Elijah seemed to collapse in fear and defeat. And herein we learn a tremendous spiritual lesson. Not only when things go badly do believers get in trouble, distress can happen after great success. In fact, success may be more dangerous than defeat.

In physics a law states for every action there is an equal and opposite reaction (Sir Isaac Newton's third law of motion). Bible students observe everything in the physical world represents a spiritual truth. Always- great spiritual successes and steps forward outrage God's enemies, both seen and unseen *Ephesians 6:12*; thus, when a believer or even a church experiences great victory or revival- be on guard for a counter spiritual attack. When Elijah heard about Jezebel's intentions, he ran for his life.

> *1 Kings 19:1-4 And Ahab told Jezebel all that Elijah had done, and withal how he had slain all the prophets with the sword. 2 Then Jezebel sent a messenger unto Elijah, saying, So let the gods do to me, and more also, if I make not thy life as the life of one of them by to morrow about this time. 3 And when he saw that, he arose, and went for his life, and came to Beersheba, which belongeth to Judah, and left his servant there.* **4 But he himself went a day's journey into the wilderness, and came and sat down under a juniper tree: and he requested for himself that he might die; and said, It is enough; now, O LORD, take away my life; for I am not better than my fathers.**

Although the mountaintop victory exhilarated Elijah and started revival, it left him exhausted and emotionally drained. Being overly tired and weary is a vulnerable time for any believer. Taking care of one's physical health can be as important as prayer and doing the Lord's work. Many mistakes are made when Christians work themselves into exhaustion. Sometimes a good rest is part of what we need. The lessons from Elijah's life are many, but one (for sure) is a person must recognize human limits of physical capability. No one is too important or too successful to fail.

1 Corinthians 10:12 *Wherefore let him that thinketh he standeth take heed lest he fall.*

Elijah sat down beneath the Juniper tree, exhausted and weary, he prayed for God to take his life. Even though the prophet felt depressed and defeated, he kept communicating to God. Have you ever felt like Elijah? Tell God exactly how you feel, rehearse all your troubles. God listens to complaints.

Although Elijah experienced huge success, the stress of the job had been too much. No matter his accomplishments, it doesn't seem good enough; the people (even God) always seem to want more. Have you ever felt like Elijah? After doing all you can, helping others to the point of personal exhaustion, only to witness ingratitude or indifference by a congregation, or even your own family? Perhaps, like Elijah, you're not aware of everything happening. Personal perceptions are not always the way things are in reality.

Notice God respects Elijah's honest prayer. God recognizes his child is emotionally falling apart. When God says *the journey is too great for thee* it is reassuring and welcoming. God understands believers can and do become overwhelmed. Although Elijah sleeps- God stays awake and nurtures his servant. The angel of the Lord remains active and ministers even while the believer is sleeping. God gives his prophet support through one meal of supernatural food- which gives him energy for forty days.

One might think after Elijah receives such intimate attention from the Lord and supernatural energy, he would be ready for battle; but this is not the case. Elijah keeps heading in the wrong direction, withdrawing not only from service, but apparently trying to hide from God. When Elijah finally stops running he takes refuge in a cave. He feels all other believers abandoned the work of the Lord. Considering his life's work futile and a failure, he sits alone and dejected in a cave. Quite a picture isn't it? Have you ever been in Elijah's cave? Are you there now?

1 Kings 19:5-9 And as he lay and slept under a juniper tree, behold, then an angel touched him, and said unto him, Arise and eat. 6 And he looked, and, behold, there was a cake baken on the coals, and a cruse of water at his head. And he did eat and drink, and laid him down again. 7 And the angel of the LORD came again the second time, and touched him, and said, Arise and eat; because the journey is too great for thee. 8 And he arose, and did eat and drink, and went in the strength of that meat forty days and forty nights unto Horeb the mount of God. 9 And he came thither unto a cave, and lodged there; and, behold, the word of the LORD came to him, and he said unto him, **What doest thou here, Elijah?**

Elijah feels alone, abandoned, hurt

The cave analogy suits many believers. Again let the reader observe the troubled saint never stops talking (praying) to God. A Christian's way back to spiritual health is through prayer and honest conversation with the Lord. When God asks Elijah what he's doing in a cave, it's like asking him, what's wrong? What problem has taken you off the battle field?

Finally, the depressed prophet opens up. He complains and explains to God exactly what's bothering him. Notice Elijah's complaint is remarkably current and up to date. He begins by stating how serious he is about serving the Lord, but then complains about the sins of his country. Next he tells God that he alone serves the Lord- no one else is doing anything. This is actually the second time Elijah voices his belief no one else cares. He expressed this same concern on top of Mount Carmel, not to God but to the people of Israel.

1 Kings 18:22 Then said Elijah unto the people, I, even I only, remain a prophet of the LORD; but Baal's prophets are four hundred and fifty men.

1 Kings 19:10 And he said, I have been very jealous for the LORD God of hosts: for the children of Israel have forsaken thy covenant, thrown down thine altars, and slain thy prophets with the sword; and I, even I only, am left; and they seek my life, to take it away.

Listening to God often requires blocking out all the noise and distractions which surround us. Once Elijah is positioned to hear, God ask him again, *What doest thou here, Elijah?*

*1 Kings 19:11-14 And he said, Go forth, and stand upon the mount before the LORD. And, behold, the LORD passed by, and a great and strong wind rent the mountains, and brake in pieces the rocks before the LORD; but the LORD was not in the wind: and after the wind an earthquake; but the LORD was not in the earthquake: 12 And after the earthquake a fire; but the LORD was not in the fire: and after the fire a still small voice. 13 And it was so, when Elijah heard it, that he wrapped his face in his mantle, and went out, and stood in the entering in of the cave. And, behold, there came a voice unto him, and said, **What doest thou here, Elijah?** 14 And he said, I have been very jealous for the LORD God of hosts: because the children of Israel have forsaken thy covenant, thrown down thine altars, and slain thy prophets with the sword; and I, even I only, am left; and they seek my life, to take it away.*

Elijah's answer remains consistent; he believes he is alone, no one else is helping. This is the third time he brings this up! God speaks in the quiet; teaching believers God inhabits caves of loneliness; answers can be found in solitude. God addresses the complaint in a significant manner. The Lord's answer is rather bitter sweet; he informs Elijah his work on earth is nearly complete (for the time being). The Lord also informs Elijah that he has been wrong in some of his conclusions.

1 Kings 19:15-18 And the LORD said unto him, Go, return on thy way to the wilderness of Damascus: and when thou comest, anoint Hazael to be king over Syria: 16 And Jehu the son of Nimshi shalt thou anoint to be king over Israel: and Elisha the son of Shaphat of Abelmeholah shalt thou anoint to be prophet in thy room. 17 And it shall come to pass, that him that escapeth the sword of Hazael shall Jehu slay: and him that escapeth from the sword of Jehu shall Elisha slay. **18 Yet I have left me seven thousand in Israel, all the knees which have not bowed unto Baal, and every mouth which hath not kissed him.**

Feeling like you are alone or the single most valuable person in God's army is self-deception. This common misperception persists amongst leadership, although rarely verbalized because it sounds so prideful; nevertheless, if the complaint fits you, listen closely to God's reply. No matter what it looks like, it is not even possible for you to see all God's servants. The Lord's plans involve far more than events going on in your life. God informs his prophet that 7,000 persons in Israel serve the Lord. This information must have shocked Elijah, because he does not know even one of them, let alone what they're doing. Let the reader ponder 7,000 individual souls with lives and situations, and troubles of their own. God works with each one. When God reveals this knowledge to Elijah, it's rather like saying: *Oh, by the way Elijah, I have 7,000 other believers so you can stop feeling like you are the only one.*

    Stressed out Bible saints have one thing in common (always), they never stop praying. Modern day believers take note. Over and over again God's people find themselves in trouble, in the midst of circumstances out of control. Suffering excruciatingly, they keep talking to God. Not with little scripted prayers, but with sincere honest, grief, hurt, and even frustrated anger.

Chapter Notes:

For Elijah's whole story and his true adventures *read 1 Kings chapters-17 through 2 Kings Chapter 3*. If you struggle maintaining interest in Bible reading, these chapters are just what you need. Elijah's adventures are thrilling and improve Christians' attention. Take time every day to read the Bible- there is no better therapy or medicine for battling tough times, depression, or sorrow. Don't believe it? Try it.

Job

§

Job 1:1-5 There was a man in the land of Uz, whose name was Job; and that man was perfect and upright, and one that feared God, and eschewed evil. 2 And there were born unto him seven sons and three daughters. 3 His substance also was seven thousand sheep, and three thousand camels, and five hundred yoke of oxen, and five hundred she asses, and a very great household; so that this man was the greatest of all the men of the east. 4 And his sons went and feasted in their houses, every one his day; and sent and called for their three sisters to eat and to drink with them. 5 And it was so, when the days of their feasting were gone about, that Job sent and sanctified them, and rose up early in the morning, and offered burnt offerings according to the number of them all: for Job said, It may be that my sons have sinned, and cursed God in their hearts. Thus did Job continually.

CONSIDERED THE OLDEST BOOK IN the Bible, Job is a book of wisdom, poetry, and advice. More than any text in the Bible, the Book of Job expounds on suffering. Although Job lived long ago, his struggle with pain is amazingly relevant. Job endures tragedy in his home, betrayal of friends and community, and feels isolated from God. Job is an extreme example of *life not being* fair. The book concludes with four full chapters of unexpected declarations from God.

Job loved the Lord and served him without hypocrisy. He was a good father, faithful to his wife, and a pillar in his community. A man of great wealth, he was generous to the poor and less fortunate. Yet God allowed Job to go through numerous tragedies. And from initial appearances, his ordeal appeared unjust, even cruel. Satan killed his ten children in a wind storm. He lost his fortune and most material goods. The people in Job's community turned against him and treated him with mockery and disdain. And if that were not enough, Job's health failed and suffered a disfiguring, painful, and seemingly terminal disease. If ever someone endured the perfect storm afflictions, it happened to Job.

God declares Job one of the best men alive, perhaps even one of the finest men who will ever live. This fact makes Job's ordeal even harder to understand. After a brief introduction describing Job, the-book opens with God engaged in a conversation with Satan. Although it may seem almost like a cruel test, careful reading shows God is in charge of the whole ordeal. God manipulates Satan to accomplish an unrevealed purpose. A very important observation is that Job remains entirely unaware of what's happening in heaven. Just like in Elijah's case, God orchestrates supernatural elements which human beings know nothing about.

> **Job 1:8** *And the LORD said unto Satan, Hast thou considered my servant Job, that there is none like him in the earth, a perfect and an upright man, one that feareth God, and escheweth evil?*

Let's examine how Job handles tragedy, and the corresponding response of his family and the community. To make this personal, imagine yourself going through an awful event. Perhaps little imagination is required? Also imagine close friends or family members going through very bad times. Why, because pain and suffering affects more than the victim. A loved one's reaction, as well as the community's response interacts significantly with tragedy. Truly pain and suffering begets pain and suffering.

JOB'S TROUBLE BEGINS:

Job 1:13-19 And there was a day when his sons and his daughters were eating and drinking wine in their eldest brother's house: 14 And there came a messenger unto Job, and said, The oxen were plowing, and the asses feeding beside them: 15 And the Sabeans fell upon them, and took them away; yea, they have slain the servants with the edge of the sword; and I only am escaped alone to tell thee. 16 While he was yet speaking, there came also another, and said, The fire of God is fallen from heaven, and hath burned up the sheep, and the servants, and consumed them; and I only am escaped alone to tell thee. 17 While he was yet speaking, there came also another, and said, The Chaldeans made out three bands, and fell upon the camels, and have carried them away, yea, and slain the servants with the edge of the sword; and I only am escaped alone to tell thee. 18 While he was yet speaking, there came also another, and said, Thy sons and thy daughters were eating and drinking wine in their eldest brother's house: 19 And, behold, there came a great wind from the wilderness, and smote the four corners of the house, and it fell upon the young men, and they are dead; and I only am escaped alone to tell thee.

RESPONSE TO TRAGEDY:

Not surprisingly, the first response comes from Job.

Job 1:20 Then Job arose, and rent his mantle, and shaved his head, and fell down upon the ground, and worshipped, 21 And said, Naked came I out of my mother's womb, and naked shall I return thither: the LORD gave, and the LORD hath taken away; blessed be the name of the LORD. 22 In all this Job sinned not, nor charged God foolishly.

As we can see, God's assessment of Job's character is vindicated. Tragedy reveals Job a remarkable individual. Initially, he accepts hard times without complaint. He is very hurt, but not bitter or angry. Not many people could suffer Job's afflictions and respond without even a hint of a *why me* attitude. Satan receives permission to deliver another devastating blow and takes Job's health.

> *Job 2:4-8 And Satan answered the LORD, and said, Skin for skin, yea, all that a man hath will he give for his life. 5 But put forth thine hand now, and touch his bone and his flesh, and he will curse thee to thy face. 6 And the LORD said unto Satan, Behold, he is in thine hand; but save his life. 7 So went Satan forth from the presence of the LORD, and smote Job with sore boils from the sole of his foot unto his crown. 8 And he took him a potsherd to scrape himself withal; and he sat down among the ashes.*

The second reaction comes from Job's wife. She seems to turn against him with her infamous quote, *curse God and die*. This, of course, adds to Job's misery. His life partner, lover, and friend isn't taking all the trouble as philosophically as her husband. She is clearly mad at God.

> *Job 2:9 Then said his wife unto him, Dost thou still retain thine integrity? curse God, and die.*

Before judging Mrs. Job, let us remember everything happening to Job in chapter1 also happened to her; an often overlooked fact. She lost her children and her fortune too. Mrs. Job went from the greatest and wealthiest woman in the East to bankruptcy in just a few days! The children's death was likely harder on the mother than the father. No doubt she grieved terribly due to her husband's sudden hideous disease. No wonder she wrestled with her faith in God. Religious men, including many ministers, regularly criticize a woman with very little consideration of her circumstances. Women often bare great suffering and stress with little understanding from family and friends. The burdens of taking care of children and maintaining a home (rarely a 50/50 proposition) go unacknowledged and underappreciated.

Job's friends

Initially Job's friends react with heartfelt compassion and absolute bewilderment at the awful tragedies afflicting their friend. Observe Job's three friends delivered their most effective help during their first week of visitation. For seven days and seven nights they said nothing. They just sat there joined in empathetic compassion for Job. Here is another important lesson on responding to a person's grief. Sometimes saying nothing is wise, being there and caring is all one should do.

> ***Job 2:11-13*** *Now when Job's three friends heard of all this evil that was come upon him, they came every one from his own place; Eliphaz the Temanite, and Bildad the Shuhite, and Zophar the Naamathite: for they had made an appointment together to come to mourn with him and to comfort him. **12** And when they lifted up their eyes afar off, and knew him not, they lifted up their voice, and wept; and they rent every one his mantle, and sprinkled dust upon their heads toward heaven. **13** So they sat down with him upon the ground seven days and seven nights, and none spake a word unto him: for they saw that his grief was very great.*

After the first week is over, however, the benefit Job received from his friends is finished. A tragedy ending quickly is one thing, quite another is an affliction that drags on and on and on. As Job's suffering continues, his friends reactions take a dark turn. Like Mrs. Job, the men start to wonder what God is doing. The problem becomes- is they think they know. We now arrive at a major theme in the book of Job and it is still a major theme in our world today.

The Book of Job is not only about one man's suffering; it is about a community's reaction to his suffering, specifically how everyone explains or justifies the tragedy. And everyone's explanation makes things worse; they become judgmental and cruel. We, like Job, live in a fallen corrupt world, yet God remains involved even when we do not understand the how, what, or why. Nevertheless, we, like Job's friends, keep trying to explain the unexplainable. Christians come up with sophisticated theology to do this: where personal sin is responsible, where Adamic sin is to blame. We talk about the perfect will of God verses the permissive will of God. But I think quite often we shout at the wind.

Christians have far more in common with Job's three friends than they do with Job.

Important lessons for Christians manifest in Job's friend's attitudes and conversations. Since we already know God considers Job upright and righteous, let us focus on the people who are not. Modern believers have far more in common with Eliphaz, Zophar, and Bildad than they do with Job, a humiliating truth seldom mentioned.

Clearly, they struggle with Job's tragedy, but even more so, they struggle with what it means to their theology. More often than not, Christians hold a preconceived idea about life. They believe certain things should not happen to believers. And when reality threatens their idealistic theology, they insist on coming up with an explanation. Very few people remain focused on the needs of others, not for very long anyway. As Job's situation drags on, the ordeal upsets their religious equilibriums, and they turn on him with ignorant vengeance. Their condemnation of Job is really a defense of what they believe about God.

A common explanation for hard times is to presume afflicted persons guilty of disobedience toward God, a standard coping method many believers embrace. Job's friends epitomize the syndrome. Behold a sampling of their remarks.

Eliphaz:

Job 4:7-9 Remember, I pray thee, who ever perished, being innocent? or where were the righteous cut off? 8 Even as I have seen, they that plow iniquity, and sow wickedness, reap the same. 9 By the blast of God they perish, and by the breath of his nostrils are they consumed.

Job 22:5-7 Is not thy wickedness great? and thine iniquities infinite? 6 For thou hast taken a pledge from thy brother for nought, and stripped the naked of their clothing. 7 Thou hast not given water to the weary to drink, and thou hast withholden bread from the hungry.

Bildad:

Job 8:5-13 If thou wouldest seek unto God betimes, and make thy supplication to the Almighty; 6 If thou wert pure and upright; surely now he would awake for thee, and make the habitation of thy righteousness prosperous. 7 Though thy beginning was small, yet thy latter end should greatly increase. 8 For inquire, I pray thee, of the former age, and prepare thyself to the search of their fathers: 9 (For we are but of yesterday, and know nothing, because our days upon earth are a shadow:) 10 Shall not they teach thee, and tell thee, and utter words out of their heart? 11 Can the rush grow up without mire? can the flag grow without water? 12 Whilst it is yet in his greenness, and not cut down, it withereth before any other herb. 13 So are the paths of all that forget God; and the hypocrite's hope shall perish:

Zophar:

Job 11:1-3 Then answered Zophar the Naamathite, and said, 2 Should not the multitude of words be answered? and should a man full of talk be justified? 3 Should thy lies make men hold their peace? and when thou mockest, shall no man make thee ashamed?

Job 20:27-29 The heaven shall reveal his iniquity; and the earth shall rise up against him. 28 The increase of his house shall depart, and his goods shall flow away in the day of his wrath. 29 This is the portion of a wicked man from God, and the heritage appointed unto him by God.

Job's friends knew he was a good man who loved the Lord, but they could not understand why God allowed this horrible sequence of calamities. They concluded it must be some kind of judgment, in other words, Job must deserve it. In order to preserve their theology, which amounted to an explanation of why God does what he does, they condemned Job. In their best efforts to explain, they stumbled in their reasoning and became physicians of no value. Like many religious people they pretend to know things they do not know. In the end, however, God condemns their theology and vindicates Job.

Job 42:7 And it was so, that after the LORD had spoken these words unto Job, the LORD said to Eliphaz the Temanite, My wrath is kindled against thee, and against thy two friends: for ye have not spoken of me the thing that is right, as my servant Job hath.

COMMUNITY REACTION

Soon the community recognizes the tragedy. Remember Job possessed great wealth and fame. His ordeal was front page news. And assessments from the world are even more callused and brutal than the church. Behold another profound yet simple lesson regarding human nature presents itself- people love a person when he's on top, but kicks him when he's down. The same community that loved Job the philanthropist, when the money ran out- turned on him without compassion. In the verses below, Job reminisced the way people treated him when he possessed wealth and high social position, and then speaks of the way people treat him in the midst of his agony and fall. Truly humans are a fickle and deceitful lot.

Job 29:21-25 Unto me men gave ear, and waited, and kept silence at my counsel. 22 After my words they spake not again; and my speech dropped upon them. 23 And they waited for me as for the rain; and they opened their mouth wide as for the latter rain. 24 If I laughed on them, they believed it not; and the light of my countenance they cast not down. 25 I chose out their way, and sat chief, and dwelt as a king in the army, as one that comforteth the mourners.

Job 30:1-14 But now they that are younger than I have me in derision, whose fathers I would have disdained to have set with the dogs of my flock. 2 Yea, whereto might the strength of their hands profit me, in whom old age was perished? 3 For want and famine they were solitary; fleeing into the wilderness in former time desolate and waste. 4 Who cut up mallows by the bushes, and juniper roots for their meat. 5 They were driven forth from among men, (they cried after them as after a thief;) 6 To dwell in the clifts of the valleys, in caves of the earth, and in the rocks. 7 Among the bushes they brayed; under the nettles they were gathered together. 8 They were children of fools, yea, children of base men: they were viler than the earth. 9 And now am I their song, yea, I am their byword. 10 They abhor me, they flee far from me, and spare not to spit in my face. 11 Because he hath loosed my cord, and afflicted me, they have also let loose the bridle before me. 12 Upon my right hand rise the youth; they push away my feet, and they raise up against me the ways of their destruction. 13 They mar my path, they set forward my calamity, they have no helper. 14 They came upon me as a wide breaking in of waters: in the desolation they rolled themselves upon me.

MODERN READER'S RESPONSE TO JOB

Today many Bible teachers and pastors explain or justify Job's ordeal by pointing out Job's self-righteousness. In other words God was teaching Job a lesson. But this rationale comes very close to doing exactly what Job's three friends were doing. When we explain Job's pain entirely based on self- righteousness, are we not echoing what Zophar, Bildad, and Eliphaz did? It seems the first response of religious people (living in any age) continues to *condemn the victim*.

No doubt scrutinizing anyone going through tragedy reveals some faults. Who among us is without sin? Who among us does not let pride interfere with serving the Lord? To justify tragedy by pointing out the sins of the victim (real or imagined) is a risky business. When it comes to an individual's personal tragedy, whether or not God's judgment has fallen- should be considered very carefully. And usually there is no way anyone can know. Empathy, prayer, and wisdom should guide the counsellor. Keep private theories to yourself unless you are scripturally armed.

Matthew 7:2-3 For with what judgment ye judge, ye shall be judged: and with what measure ye mete, it shall be measured to you again. 3 And why beholdest thou the mote that is in thy brother's eye, but considerest not the beam that is in thine own eye?

Job summarizes his own righteousness in chapters 29 and 30. These chapters fuel the popular theological position that Job deserves what he gets. To be sure Job perceived his high moral standing, and his own words paint a rather lofty self-portrait, but let us not forget God declared him one of the best men who ever lived. So if Job being self-righteous is the reason God put him through the pain, then what do regular men and women deserve? Job's self-righteousness accusation is overplayed.

Like Job's friends- modern readers know Job was a good man, but we wrestle with why God let Satan torment him. In order to preserve our theology, do we conclude Job deserved it? Are we quick to blame the victim when we see good people suffering today? In our best efforts to explain, do we stumble in our reasoning? When it comes to comforting those in pain, are we also physicians of no value?

> *Job 13:3-4 Surely I would speak to the Almighty, and I desire to reason with God. 4 But ye are forgers of lies, ye are all physicians of no value.*

Condemning the victim is not the only method used by believers. When faced with situations seemingly incompatible with a loving and kind God, believers often imagine bizarre theories as to why tragedies occur. A comforter who says the wrong thing (with the best of intentions) is common.

I remember the week we received the awful news about our daughter's brain disease. A dear friend of my wife approached her at church and said, "Now you know why God just gave you another daughter who is healthy? God knew this was going to happen. Isn't the Lord wonderful?" (A few months earlier, our youngest daughter had been born) With the best and kindest intent, a very uncomforting remark was made. In reality my wife's friend tried to make her own beliefs make sense about why bad things happen. Equally without wisdom was the consoling interpretation given to me by yet another friend. I was told, since we were patient and caring parents, God knew we could handle a handicapped child. Apparently, to this fellow, our perceived good standing in Christ rewarded us with a sick child. And, of course, anyone experiencing tragedy can always expect someone to quote *Romans 8:28.*

> *Romans 8:28 And we know that all things work together for good to them that love God, to them who are the called according to his purpose.*

Certainly the verse applies to agonizing situations, but there is an appropriate time to present it. Christians should comfort others with careful consideration of what they say and when they say it. Imagine yourself going through the same anguish as the person you are about to console. What would make you feel better? Compassion and wisdom need to walk together- unfortunately, often they do not.

Isaiah 50:4 The Lord GOD hath given me the tongue of the learned, that I should know how to speak a word in season to him that is weary: he wakeneth morning by morning, he wakeneth mine ear to hear as the learned.

Proverbs 25:11 A word fitly spoken is like apples of gold in pictures of silver.

When Things Get Worse

§

Psalms 13:1 To the chief Musician, A Psalm of David. How long wilt thou forget me, O LORD? for ever? how long wilt thou hide thy face from me?

As STATED EARLIER, A BRIEF tragic episode is one thing; it is quite another when the pain and suffering continues for long periods of time. For example, the sudden death of a loved one is painful, but watching a loved one suffer from a debilitating, painful disease- month after month, year after year- may be much worse. Or if one loses a job for a few months it makes things financially difficult; however, if one remains unemployed for an extended period of time- it can be devastating.

Although Job continues to love God, he descends ever deeper into despair and frustration. Trouble takes a serious spiritual toll. Job becomes the first (documented) great believer whose pain and suffering so exhausts him he actually considers death more desirable than living.

Job 3:1-5 After this opened Job his mouth, and cursed his day. 2 And Job spake, and said, 3 Let the day perish wherein I was born, and the night in which it was said, There is a man child conceived. 4 Let that day be darkness; let not God regard it from above, neither let the light shine upon it. 5 Let darkness and the shadow of death stain it; let a cloud dwell upon it; let the blackness of the day terrify it.

Job 17:11-16 My days are past, my purposes are broken off, even the thoughts of my heart. 12 They change the night into day: the light is short because of darkness. 13 If I wait, the grave is mine house: I have made my bed in the darkness. 14 I have said to corruption, Thou art my father: to the worm, Thou art my mother, and my sister. 15 And where is now my hope? as for my hope, who shall see it? 16 They shall go down to the bars of the pit, when our rest together is in the dust.

Job reaches the point where he believes happiness is no longer possible. Job mistakenly concludes his earthly life offers nothing more than misery, but Job does not know the future. In just a short time, Job's life will turn from agony to blessing. The same may be true for modern day suffering believers. Simply not knowing the future can be hopeful.

Observe even in Job's darkest hour, he never forgets his eternal destiny. His hope is heaven. Just think when Job spoke these words in desperate prayer, he had no idea God wrote them down. Job's insight into the resurrection proves he believed in life after death. He also believed God provides believers new immortal bodies. Likewise, whatever tragedy modern believers face today, and even if it appears hopeless, the knowledge of an eternal heaven is still truth. Thus an eternal weight of glory works for good in the worst afflictions.

Job 19:23-29 Oh that my words were now written! oh that they were printed in a book! 24 That they were graven with an iron pen and lead in the rock for ever! 25 For I know that my redeemer liveth, and that he shall stand at the latter day upon the earth: 26 And though after my skin worms destroy this body, yet in my flesh shall I see God: ***27*** *Whom I shall see for myself, and mine eyes shall behold, and not another; though my reins be consumed within me.* ***28*** *But ye should say, Why persecute we him, seeing the root of the matter is found in me?* ***29*** *Be ye afraid of the sword: for wrath bringeth the punishments of the sword, that ye may know there is a judgment.*

A bit of trivia: The inventor of the printing press, **Johannes Gutenberg** (1398 AD-1468 AD) found inspiration in *Job 19:23-24* for his invention of movable type- revolutionizing printing. The first book printed from this system was the Bible.

Closing Thoughts

Believers are being formed and shaped by God to live in heaven. Our Creator continues to create us even as we live. Just as an artist uses colors and techniques to paint a picture, so does Jesus use life experiences to accomplish his perfect will in us. Pain and suffering are colors on our creator's pallet. These colors include numerous shades and hues.

Distress does something to a developing soul that nothing else can do. Why God chooses some people to suffer more than others is a question I cannot answer. But this I do know: The Bible records numerous accounts of believers living in grief. Those stories profoundly affect the lives of other people in a very positive manner. As we read about the agony of Job, Elijah, and Jeremiah (to name a few) - how is it their anguish causes us to grow spiritually? Not that we delight in their suffering, but their testimonies and struggles connect us in powerful ways. How does your suffering affect the lives of others? You have no idea; only eternity will tell.

In 1,500 BC Moses declared man's life span to be 70 years, perhaps a little longer? That's not a lot of time, middle age is 35. Moses also told us we live our lives as a tale that is told. Think about all the stories of men and women in the Bible. They had no idea that God wrote their lives as chapters to be scrutinized and studied by future believers. Perhaps our tales will be read by believers thousands of years from now? (A rather uncomfortable thought.) What God does with your story only eternity knows.

> **Psalms 90:9-10** *For all our days are passed away in thy wrath: we spend our years as a tale that is told. 10 The days of our years are threescore years and ten; and if by reason of strength they be fourscore years, yet is their strength labour and sorrow; for it is soon cut off, and we fly away.*

Many situations cannot be understood this side of heaven. Let us pray God gives us wisdom to trust him. Faith, hope, and charity remain powerful weapons in the battle against anguish and pain. Through faith and hope, we know God is good, and he will give us an eternity of happiness. Through charity, we can choose to give all we can to others. I believe God comprehends human suffering on two levels. God feels the pain and anguish of each individual, and he comprehends all human agonies collectively with empathy only the omnipotent God could endure.

> **Isaiah 53:3-4** *He is despised and rejected of men; a man of sorrows, and acquainted with grief: and we hid as it were our faces from him; he was despised, and we esteemed him not. 4 Surely he hath borne our griefs, and carried our sorrows: yet we did esteem him stricken, smitten of God, and afflicted.*

The history of Christianity is well documented. For the last 2,000 years the Bride's joy and her pain fill many books. How tortured Christians entertained ancient Roman crowds. How, through hundreds of years called the dark ages, mankind suffered terribly from plagues, famine, and persecution. The Protestant Reformation brought millions to Christ, but once again Rome tried to stamp out the truth. In her unsuccessful wake, she left tens of thousands maimed and dead.

Suffering and pain exist within the body of Christ. Those who can't see it are preoccupied with themselves; those who deny it choose fantasy. Unless we are raptured, our future here ends in hospital beds and graveyards. Every day we enjoy on earth is due to God's mercy and his grace. Health and well-being are blessings from God; they are not things we demand. All creation waits for deliverance from pain.

> *Isaiah 35:5-6 Then the eyes of the blind shall be opened, and the ears of the deaf shall be unstopped. 6 Then shall the lame man leap as an hart, and the tongue of the dumb sing: for in the wilderness shall waters break out, and streams in the desert.*

> *Revelation 21:4 And God shall wipe away all tears from their eyes; and there shall be no more death, neither sorrow, nor crying, neither shall there be any more pain: for the former things are passed away.*

Chapter Notes

> *Romans 8:28-29 And we know that all things work together for good to them that love God, to them who are the called according to his purpose. 29 For whom he did foreknow, he also did predestinate to be conformed to the image of his Son, that he might be the first-born among many brethren.*

> *Romans 12:2 And be not conformed to this world: but be ye transformed by the renewing of your mind, that ye may prove what is that good, and acceptable, and perfect, will of God.*

Galatians 4:19 *My little children, of whom I travail in birth again until Christ be formed in you,*

Isaiah 64:8 *But now, O LORD, thou art our father; we are the clay, and thou our potter; and we all are the work of thy hand.*

God's Response

§

Job 38:2 Who is this that darkeneth counsel by words without knowledge?

THE CULMINATION OF THE BOOK of Job is startling. In chapters 38-41 God speaks directly to Job. Ponder prayerfully how God concludes the Book of Job. Enough content in these chapters exist for commentators to write thousands of books-I attempt to touch but a tiny portion as it relates to the topic of suffering.

Unbeknown to Job, God was very mindful and involved throughout his whole ordeal. The Lord listened intently to all his friends' comments, their theories, and attempts to speak in God's behalf. He also listened to Job's agonies, his self-defense, his complaints, and worship. And now God speaks. Clearly God is addressing Job, but don't forget, four other people remain in audience. No doubt all men listened to God's voice with awe and terror.

Job 38:1-4Then the LORD answered Job out of the whirlwind, and said, **2 Who is this that darkeneth counsel by words without knowledge?** *3 Gird up now thy loins like a man; for I will demand of thee, and answer thou me.4 Where wast thou when I laid the foundations of the earth? declare, if thou hast understanding.*

God's first statement is a question to all present, and all future readers (and commentators) of Job's ordeal. *Who is this that darkeneth counsel by words without knowledge?* Quite a rebuke is it not? Just imagine those four men, so sure of themselves explaining God's intentions. Methinks the question remains pertinent today. So much of what people say is just talk founded upon private interpretation and theological theories.

The question sets the tenor for what follows. God states question after question no human being could possibly answer. He also declares unknown facts on everything from the origin of the universe to distant galaxies and stellar constellations to earth's meteorological phenomena. Obviously; compared to God's wisdom- man knows almost nothing.

In quiet awe Job listens. When Job finally answers, he speaks with absolute humility, and submission; without even a hint of self-righteousness. Job instantly responds with self-loathing and repentance. He refers to himself as vile and basically says he has nothing to say. When believers draw close to God, there is an overwhelming sense of God's holiness and power.

> *Job 40:3-8 3 Then Job answered the LORD, and said, 4 Behold, I am vile; what shall I answer thee? I will lay mine hand upon my mouth. 5 Once have I spoken; but I will not answer: yea, twice; but I will proceed no further.*

When it comes to passing judgment on people, Job teaches important truths. Truly, while speaking to his friends, Job announced his own righteousness. But in the presence of God he has nothing to say. Christians should remember, it's one thing for God to judge a man and quite another when other believers do the judging. Since God considers Job one of his best- there is no use in the rest of us bragging about anything. I am persuaded the primary message in the Book of Job is the presumptive arrogance believers' demonstrate as they attempt to explain why bad things happen to good people.

As to why Job went through his terrible ordeal, God selected him to do so. Considering God concluded the whole episode with four chapters displaying his own vast intellect and abilities contrasted to the pitiful ignorance of human beings, I think it more than foolishness to comment further.

> **Romans 11:33-34** *O the depth of the riches both of the wisdom and knowledge of God! how unsearchable are his judgments, and his ways past finding out!* **34** *For who hath known the mind of the Lord? or who hath been his counseller?*

> **Isaiah 55:8-9** *For my thoughts are not your thoughts, neither are your ways my ways, saith the LORD.* **9** *For as the heavens are higher than the earth, so are my ways higher than your ways, and my thoughts than your thoughts.*

end

Backsliding

§

Proverbs 14:14 *The backslider in heart*
shall be filled with his own ways: and a good
man shall be satisfied from himself.

No Christian obtains anything close to moral perfection this side
of heaven. Being satisfied or delivered from oneself is a great promise. As
mentioned earlier, Christians face two kinds of afflictions in life. The environmental which includes all griefs out of our control, and the affliction
which Christians brings upon themselves through disobedience. Sinful
behavior brings untold miseries and unhappiness to many a wayward pil-
grim. This book would be remiss without a chapter on backsliding.

> *Psalms 119:67* *Before I was afflicted I went astray: but now have*
> *I kept thy word.*

> *Psalms 119:75* *I know, O LORD, that thy judgments are right,*
> *and that thou in faithfulness hast afflicted me.*

> *Jeremiah 17:9* *The heart is deceitful above all things, and desper-*
> *ately wicked: who can know it?*

Ponder the percentage of sermons categorized under the topic: *How*
should we then live? The preacher encourages righteous living while

condemning his flock's sinful behaviors. How many Bible verses amount to listing things we should resist, and things we should be doing? Why tell Christians not to lie, unless we are prone to lying. Why warn about gossiping, worldly living, drinking, swearing, pride, fornications, thefts, (enough the list is endless).

Acknowledging the sins of others is tolerable, but making it personal is uncomfortable. With ease I judge others; with determined reluctance I judge myself.

Matthew 7:3 And why beholdest thou the mote that is in thy brother's eye, but considerest not the beam that is in thine own eye?

Romans 2:21-22 Thou therefore which teachest another, teachest thou not thyself? thou that preachest a man should not steal, dost thou steal? 22 Thou that sayest a man should not commit adultery, dost thou commit adultery? thou that abhorrest idols, dost thou commit sacrilege?

Salvation's first evidence is conviction of sins. The Holy Ghost presses upon believers the shame and evil of unrighteousness. Personally, I remember how things I once enjoyed doing, suddenly made me feel guilty. In other words, Jesus ruined the party. No matter how many times I tried to regain sins' pleasure, gratification like the way it used to be- was gone. Even though my flesh determined to have it so, the Holy Spirit condemned me for doing it. Whether done in private or in the open, nothing was the same. Shamefully, I held on far too long to things that needed dismissed. Likewise I resisted God's instruction. I am well qualified to write this chapter. I often muse, more seriously than not, when Apostle Paul wrote his famous self-evaluation, that I had not been born yet.

1 Timothy 1:15 This is a faithful saying, and worthy of all acceptation, that Christ Jesus came into the world to save sinners; of whom I am chief.

John 16:8 *And when he is come, he will reprove the world of sin, and of righteousness, and of judgment:*

Lot: Testimonial Power

The Bible records several backsliders. God never covers up sin. For our instruction and learning, examining their lives is expedient. Consider Lot and his residence in Sodom. Lot believed in God and partook of Abraham's blessing. In the New Testament, scripture reveals Lot vexed his righteous soul every day because he lived in Sodom.

> ***2 Peter 2:6-8*** *And turning the cities of Sodom and Gomorrha into ashes condemned them with an overthrow, making them an ensample unto those that after should live ungodly; 7 And delivered just Lot, vexed with the filthy conversation of the wicked: 8 (For that righteous man dwelling among them, in seeing and hearing, vexed his righteous soul from day to day with their unlawful deeds;)*

God's reference to Lot's character *in 2 Peter,* illuminates backsliding in a significant way. The trouble with Lot is he chose to live in Sodom. Without describing Sodom's social activities, let us view the damage. *Biblical history overtly records the city's reputation.* If ever a city equated with sin, it was Sodom. Lot even sat in the gate, which means he involved himself in the city's commerce and politics; alas, Lot made money there.

To put the reader in remembrance, sin reached such an intolerable level in Sodom, God sent two angels to destroy the city. God's mercy warned Lot and his family judgment was coming, and offered them deliverance. Lot understood all this very well. These angels weren't fooling around; judgment was imminent. In desperation, Lot gathered his immediate family and ran down the street to warn his daughters and sons-in-law. And it is at this juncture in the scriptural narrative when tragedy strikes the heart of Lot- and the hearts of all backsliders. At that moment, what Lot needed more than anything he ever needed in his life was a good testimony; and he did not have one; he owned a bad testimony. Consequently, no one believed what Lot said, including people he loved. Tragically, Lot's loved ones and friends perished in God's ensuing judgment.

> **Genesis 19:12-14** *And the men said unto Lot, Hast thou here any besides? son in law, and thy sons, and thy daughters, and whatsoever thou hast in the city, bring them out of this place:* **13** *For we will destroy this place, because the cry of them is waxen great before the face of the LORD; and the LORD hath sent us to destroy it.* **14** *And Lot went out, and spake unto his sons in law, which married his daughters, and said, Up, get you out of this place; for the LORD will destroy this city.* **But he seemed as one that mocked unto his sons in law.**

* **Mocked** definition: tease or laugh at in a scornful or contemptuous manner. Ridicule, jeer, make fun of. Make something seem laughable, unreal, and impossible.

Every believer earns a testimony. We can only wonder how backslidden Lot was- Did he drink what his fellow citizens drank? Did he smoke what they did? Did he swear like them? Did he partake in the same entertainment and frequent the same shows? Where and how did he make his money? All that mattered, however, is the people who knew him best thought he was joking when he talked about God. In fact, they thought he mocked. Of course they based this on how they saw Lot live. Let Christians ponder this was not believers judging him, this was the world's conclusion.

A sobering truth dear Christian, is you are the best Christian somebody knows. And it does not matter if you are a good or bad Christian. For some lost people, when they think about Jesus Christ, they think of you. Almost cliché but the truth is profound; you are the only Bible many people read. God entrusts all Christians with this tremendous unsearchable eternal weight of glory.

KING JEHOSHAPHAT: COMPROMISING VALUES

Compromising values and worldly alliances. Many Christians join forces with the world for gain, be it personal or for the group. This kind of backsliding is rather subtle and less intentional than open rebellion, but never the less, causes much damage. If done by leadership, it wounds an entire church, organization, or country. Studying King Jehoshaphat provides excellent information for those who backslide with good intentions, the end justifies the means kind of rationale.

King Jehoshaphat, was a good king of Judah who loved the Lord. Under threat of war, he made an alliance with Israel's wicked King Ahab. The strategy designed as a temporary military alliance to defeat a common enemy. Jehoshaphat also hoped (naively) to persuade King Ahab to serve the true God. He wanted to be a good witness. Because both nations shared a common heritage, Jehoshaphat hoped to unite the countries.

Several generations earlier, God divided Israel into two nations, Israel and Judah. The nation Judah followed the Lord, but Israel fell into gross idolatry and had only gotten worse since the division. King Ahab and his notorious Queen Jezebel served the false god, Baal and sought to kill the Lord's prophets. Israel never intended to stop its evil ways. Any compromising, would be done by Jehoshaphat not Ahab.

*2 Chronicles 18:1-4 Now Jehoshaphat had riches and honour in abundance, **and joined affinity with Ahab**. 2 And after certain years he went down to Ahab to Samaria. And Ahab killed sheep and oxen for him in abundance, and for the people that he had with* *him, and persuaded him to go up with him to Ramothgilead. 3 And Ahab king of Israel said unto Jehoshaphat king of Judah, Wilt thou go with me to Ramothgilead?* **And he answered him, I am as thou art, and my people as thy people; and we will be with thee in the war.** *4 And Jehoshaphat said unto the king of Israel, Inquire, I pray thee, at the word of the LORD to day.*

The problem was Jehoshaphat's people were not like Ahab's people. Jehoshaphat deluded himself and created an alliance God opposed. With a very royal and public ceremony, the two kings sat side by side. Jehoshaphat even endured listening to false prophets lie and encourage battle plans. The lesson learned from this fiasco - when Christians join forces with the world, it is Christians who compromise values- the world never does.

2 Chronicles 18:5-9 Therefore the king of Israel gathered together of prophets four hundred men, and said unto them, Shall we go to Ramothgilead to battle, or shall I forbear? And they said, Go up; for God will deliver it into the king's hand. 6 But Jehoshaphat said, Is there not here a prophet of the LORD besides, that we might inquire of him? 7 And the king of Israel said unto Jehoshaphat, **There is yet one man, by whom we may inquire of the LORD: but I hate him;** *for he never prophesied good unto me, but always evil: the same is Micaiah the son of Imla. And Jehoshaphat said, Let not the king say so. 8 And the king of Israel called for one of his officers, and said, Fetch quickly Micaiah the son of Imla.* **9 And the king of Israel and Jehoshaphat king of Judah sat either of them on his throne, clothed in their robes, and they sat in a void place at the entering in of the gate of Samaria; and all the prophets prophesied before them.**

Jehoshaphat's alliance with Ahab is one of the most extraordinary backsliding events in the Bible. This momentary poor choice produces ramifications for the next 150 years. Satan was the author of this whole deal, confusing and mixing up Judah and Israel so effectively that even historians have trouble sorting it all out.

In his zeal to defeat a common enemy, the first thing Jehoshaphat didn't see coming involved family. Accompanying Jehoshaphat during the notorious alliance ceremony was his teenage son, Jehoram. Also in attendance, across the aisle, was Ahab's and Jezebel's daughter, Athaliah. Well- the sweet young Israeli princess fancied the handsome young prince from Judah. And after the flirting stopped, the true joining of nations took place. Nothing like forbidden love, especially when Satan orchestrates courtship for future kings and queens. More about this later.

But in the meantime, the battle is upon them. Ahab took charge of the battle plans and instructs Jehoshaphat to dress in overt royal clothing, so all soldiers can easily identify him as king. While Ahab dresses in common soldier attire. How a good king like Jehoshaphat could be so duped is quite fascinating. Perhaps Ahab's personality dominated him, or perhaps he pitched the plan so it made sense? Who knows? Anyone can make a mistake. Thankfully, God protected Jehoshaphat. King Ahab's incognito uniform proved useless and he was killed in the battle.

2 Chronicles 18:28-34 So the king of Israel and Jehoshaphat the king of Judah went up to Ramothgilead. **29 And the king of Israel said unto Jehoshaphat, I will disguise myself, and will go to the battle; but put thou on thy robes.** *So the king of Israel disguised himself; and they went to the battle. 30 Now the king of Syria had commanded the captains of the chariots that were with him, saying, Fight ye not with small or great, save only with the king of Israel. 31 And it came to pass, when the captains of the chariots saw Jehoshaphat, that they said, It is the king of Israel. Therefore they compassed about him to fight: but Jehoshaphat cried* *out, and the LORD helped him; and God moved them to depart from him. 32 For it came to pass, that, when the captains of the chariots perceived that it was not the king of Israel, they turned back again from pursuing him. 33 And a certain man drew a bow at a venture, and smote the king of Israel between the joints of the harness: therefore he said to his chariot man, Turn thine hand, that thou mayest carry me out of the host; for I am wounded. 34* ***And the battle increased that day: howbeit the king of Israel stayed himself up in his chariot against the Syrians until the even: and about the time of the sun going down he died.***

Unbeknown to either king, Satan used them both in a supernaturally brilliant scheme. God declared Satan perfect in wisdom and the author of confusion; and the old serpent certainly earns his titles here. Believers do well to obey God always, even when it looks like a little compromising is a good idea. God's people can make wrong decisions; it happens frequently. Satan probably wanted Ahab dead; his big plans involved future generations. But consider what would have happened if Jehoshaphat died in the battle, like Ahab wanted.

1. After the alliance ceremony, Ahab would have tried to be Judah's king.
2. Ahab's god was not God.
3. You should not join forces with the ungodly to battle a common enemy.

Eventually Jehoshaphat's son marries Athaliah. So now Judah and Israel are united through royal marriage. Satan successfully mixes a cursed kingdom with a blessed kingdom.

Generations later, (long after Jehoshaphat dies) Athaliah now a grandmother to the kingdom of Judah's genetically linked line of David's children- murders all but one son in line for the throne. Needless to say Satan tried to destroy all the seed of David with the ultimate goal of stopping the coming Messiah. Not until King Herod, murders all children under two years of age (700 years later in the New Testament) will there be a more nefarious attack on the line of David.

With the death of Ahab and Jehoshaphat- national confusion ensues. So much so even Bible historians argue about the situation. Without discussing all the confusion, observe just some of the tragic ramifications from one backslidden decision.

*2 **Chronicles** 22:1-4 And the inhabitants of Jerusalem made Ahaziah his youngest son king in his stead: for the band of men that came with the Arabians to the camp had slain all the eldest. So Ahaziah the son of Jehoram king of Judah reigned. **2** Forty and two years old was Ahaziah when he began to reign, and he reigned one year in Jerusalem.* **His mother's name also was Athaliah the daughter of Omri. 3 He also walked in the ways of the house of Ahab: for his mother was his counseller to do wickedly. 4 Wherefore he did evil in the sight of the LORD like the house of Ahab: for they were his counsellers after the death of his father to his destruction.**

*2 **Chronicles** 22:10* **But when Athaliah the mother of Ahaziah saw that her son was dead, she arose and destroyed all the seed royal of the house of Judah.** *11 But Jehoshabeath, the daughter of the king, took Joash the son of Ahaziah, and stole him from among the king's sons that were slain, and put him and his nurse in a bedchamber. So Jehoshabeath, the daughter of king Jehoram, the wife of Jehoiada the priest, (for she was the sister of Ahaziah,) hid him from Athaliah, so that she slew him not. 12 And he was with them hid in the house of God six years: and Athaliah reigned over the land.*

King David:

Everyone wants what they can't have.
King David served the Lord with all his heart. The Lord honors him and actually equates his name with doing well. But with a momentary distraction, he fell morally. He sees a beautiful woman, Bathsheba, and lusts. Arranging things so as to accommodate a meeting, the deed is done.

Nearly everyone knows about King David and his adulterous affair with Bathsheba. And I do mean everyone in the world,- even in modern times! This fact alone is worthy of consideration. When a believer falls into sin, the world loves it. And the more important or famous the backslider- the bigger the celebration. To this day, Hollywood makes movies about King David's adultery, while ignoring all his righteous and wonderful accomplishments. *Nothing quite like a hot scandal committed by those hypocritical Christians.*

When Christians fail morally it's comforting to lost people. Why? Because it makes them less nervous about their own judgment. Hence the logical argument, *if believers live in sin, what's the difference between me and them? Since they're lying about righteous living- the salvation argument must not be true either.*

Another pertinent point to the Christian backslider is everyone wants what they shouldn't have. Nothing is ever enough. Kings enjoy multiple wives, concubines, and usually harems. Still they are not satisfied. Why? Because, even after salvation, a believer's flesh remains at war with righteousness. Be you king or pauper, if you let your guard down you fall. In many areas: power, sex, possessions, money, etc. our flesh remains insatiable, no matter what you own or accomplish.

1 Corinthians 10:12 *Wherefore let him that thinketh he standeth take heed lest he fall.*

1 John 2:16 For all that is in the world, the lust of the flesh, and the lust of the eyes, and the pride of life, is not of the Father, but is of the world.

Galatians 5:19-21 Now the works of the flesh are manifest, which are these; Adultery, fornication, uncleanness, lasciviousness, 20 Idolatry, witchcraft, hatred, variance, emulations, wrath, strife, seditions, heresies, 21 Envyings, murders, drunkenness, revellings, and such like: of the which I tell you before, as I have also told you in time past, that they which do such things shall not inherit the kingdom of God.

Scripture identifies the time David committed adultery as *when kings go forth to battle.* Observe David was not where he belonged. What is David doing at the palace? Sin usually requires opportunity. If believers occupy themselves in what they should be doing, opportunities to backslide diminish. Not completely, but it helps.

After their encounter, Bathsheba is pregnant. David tries to avoid responsibility by bringing her husband, Uriah, home from battle. Nothing like some rest, relaxation and a conjugal evening with one's wife to ease the stress of war. This, of course, would make Bathsheba's pregnancy look respectable. As fate has it, however, Uriah happens to be the noblest guy in the king's army. Selfless and thinking only about the war, he refuses to enjoy pleasure with his wife while his army brothers engage in battle; Uriah seeks only returning to soldier's duty. In desperation, David sends a letter to Joab, his general, with orders for Uriah to get killed in battle. An often overlooked condition is the letter sentences numerous soldiers' deaths. David's murderous scheme is getting worse. Sin always compounds itself.

2 Samuel 11:1-17 And it came to pass, after the year was expired, at the time when kings go forth to battle, that David sent Joab, and his servants with him, and all Israel; and they destroyed the children of Ammon, and besieged Rabbah. **But David tarried still at Jerusalem. 2 And it came to pass in an eveningtide, that David arose from off his bed, and walked upon the roof of the king's house: and from the roof he saw a woman washing herself; and the woman was very beautiful to look upon.** *3 And David sent and inquired after the woman. And one said, Is not this Bathsheba, the daughter of Eliam, the wife of Uriah the Hittite? 4 And David sent messengers, and took her; and she came in unto him, and he lay with her; for she was purified from her uncleanness: and she returned unto her house. 5 And the woman conceived, and sent and told David, and said, I am with child. 6 And David sent to Joab, saying, Send me Uriah the Hittite. And Joab sent Uriah to David. 7 And when Uriah was come unto him, David demanded of him how Joab did, and how the people did, and how the war prospered. 8 And David said to Uriah, Go down to thy house, and wash thy feet. And Uriah departed out of the king's house, and there followed him a mess of meat from the king. 9 But Uriah slept at the door of the king's house with all the servants of his lord, and went not down to his house. 10 And when they had told David, saying, Uriah went not down unto his house, David said unto Uriah, Camest thou not from thy journey? why then didst thou not go down unto thine house?* **11 And Uriah said unto David, The ark, and Israel, and Judah, abide in tents; and my lord Joab, and the servants of my lord, are encamped in the open fields; shall I then go into mine house, to eat and to drink, and to lie with my wife? as thou livest, and as thy soul liveth, I will not do this thing.** *12 And David said to Uriah, Tarry here to day also, and to morrow I will let thee depart. So Uriah abode in Jerusalem that day, and the morrow. 13 And when David had called him, he did eat and drink before him; and he made him drunk: and at even he went out to lie on his bed with the servants of his lord, but went not down to his house. 14 And it came to pass in the morning, that David wrote a letter to Joab,* *and sent it by the hand of Uriah. 15 And he wrote in the letter, saying, Set ye Uriah in the forefront of the hottest battle, and retire ye from him, that he may be smitten, and die. 16 And it came to pass, when Joab observed the city, that he assigned Uriah unto a place where he knew that valiant men were. 17 And the men of the city went out, and fought with Joab: and there fell some of the people of the servants of David; and Uriah the Hittite died also.*

The Shame of Backsliding

Another major fact about backsliding. The cover-up never works. Quite often the sins committed trying to cover the first sins are worse than the original acts. Be sure your sin will find you out. *Numbers 32:23*

Some people's backsliding remains hidden for a long time, perhaps decades, but in the end nothing escapes God's watchful eye. Whether one's sins parade through the media, the church, family, or the Judgment Seat of Christ; it will be exposed. Don't deceive yourself.

> *Ecclesiastes 8:11 Because sentence against an evil work is not executed speedily, therefore the heart of the sons of men is fully set in them to do evil.*

Believers learn an important lesson from the way David handles repentance. The king is grieved, and not just because he gets caught. The fact his sin grieves God grieves David. Unrighteousness and sin brings sorrow to true believers, if it doesn't the sinner is not saved. If professed believers enjoy sin without God's conviction, and their main concern is getting caught- the believers are frauds. From little lies to murder- God hates sin.

2 Corinthians 13:5 Examine yourselves, whether ye be in the faith; prove your own selves. Know ye not your own selves, how that Jesus Christ is in you, except ye be reprobates?

Ephesians 4:30 And grieve not the holy Spirit of God, whereby ye are sealed unto the day of redemption.

Once David admits and repents, God gives mercy. And this is exactly what Christians may expect when they admit and repent from backsliding. Yet damage is done. In David's case tremendous consequences ensued: soldiers died and their families knew why, the whole kingdom knew, David's sins delighted the enemies of God, a baby died, and future family problems occur.

2 Samuel 12:13-14 And David said unto Nathan, I have sinned against the LORD. And Nathan said unto David, The LORD also hath put away thy sin; thou shalt not die. **14 Howbeit, because by this deed thou hast given great occasion to the enemies of the LORD to blaspheme, the child also that is born unto thee shall surely die.**

1 John 1:9 If we confess our sins, he is faithful and just to forgive us our sins, and to cleanse us from all unrighteousness.

Psalms 38:18 For I will declare mine iniquity; I will be sorry for my sin.

Proverbs 28:13 He that covereth his sins shall not prosper: but whoso confesseth and forsaketh them shall have mercy.

Ephesians 4:30 And grieve not the holy Spirit of God, whereby ye are sealed unto the day of redemption.

King Solomon: Backsliding Doesn't Work

When it comes to backsliding, the posterchild is King Solomon. A true believer who loved God, yet he spent years of his life in relapsed misery. This study focuses on the spiritual fruit of backsliding. In other words, what does the believer get from rebellion? Studying Solomon also ponders why some believers continue to backslide throughout their life.

Solomon is the epitome of the man who has everything. As King David's son, he grew up in royal privilege. Upon taking the Israel's throne, he made a selfless and important prayer to God. His prayer expressed humility. Solomon asked for understanding and wise discernment, so he could lead the Lord's people.

> *1 Kings 3:10-13 And the speech pleased the Lord, that Solomon had asked this thing. 11 And God said unto him, Because thou hast asked this thing, and hast not asked for thyself long life; neither hast asked riches for thyself, nor hast asked the life of thine enemies; but hast asked for thyself understanding to discern judgment; 12 Behold, I have done according to thy words: lo, I have given thee a wise and an understanding heart; so that there was none like thee before thee, neither after thee shall any arise like unto thee. 13 And I have also given thee that which thou hast not asked, both riches, and honour: so that there shall not be any among the kings like unto thee all thy days.*

God gave Solomon more than anyone ever dreamed. God's gifts to Solomon make him the perfect subject for a study on backsliding. No one who ever lived compares to Solomon, including modern day billionaires, kings, or presidents. King Solomon's possessed far more than worldly goods. Being the most understanding, wisest, and knowledgeable human being conveys staggering cognitive, philosophical, scientific, and spiritual abilities. Comparing him to the entire human race (then and now) King Solomon was the following:

1. The wisest man.
2. The most knowledgeable (smartest) man.
3. The richest man.
4. The most powerful man.

These things established, Solomon started off well. God used him to write the Bible's wisdom books, Proverbs, Ecclesiastes, Song of Solomon. But King Solomon took a wrong turn in life. He rebelled and sought satisfaction apart from God. And he sought fulfillment in all areas: science, spiritual, philosophy, religion, and flesh. Nothing was left untried. King Solomon's evaluation of backsliding merits our scrutiny. Let us consider what the wisest person God every made says about sin.

Solomon's dark journey into sin causes more than a few Bible students to wonder if the rebellious king went to heaven or hell. My personal answer to the question is heaven. Perhaps the salient reason the Lord endured King Solomon excursion to the dark side was for his explanation to all believers why they should not do it?

The book Ecclesiastes sums up the foolishness and mistakes of backsliding, there is no book like it in the entire Bible. Immediately Ecclesiastes opens with Solomon's conclusions about life; the signature statement from the dark king. A conclusion Solomon rehearses over and over again.

Ecclesiastes 1:1-2 *The words of the Preacher, the son of David, king in Jerusalem.* **2 Vanity of vanities, saith the Preacher, vanity of vanities; all is vanity.**

Since Solomon uses the word vanity so often, it behooves Christians to research vanity's full depth. Along with the dictionary' definition, we must observe the context in which Solomon consistently employs the word. Bible students refer to this as letting scripture interpret scripture, or the Bible is its own best dictionary.

We begin by defining the word vain (root of vanity)

1. Having no real value: idle, worthless
2. Marked by futility or ineffectualness

Vanity manifests emptiness, or valueless, the quality or fact of being vain. Psychologically vanity can develop into extreme selfishness, with a grandiose view of one's own talents and a craving for admiration.

Biblically, I am convinced the definition must also include deception. **Vanity=Deception**. Deception steadfastly remains essential to scripturally comprehending backsliding.

Lest anyone doubt the smartest man, or suppose God withdrew his supernatural wisdom by removing Holy Ghost influence. Observe God instructed Solomon to write that wisdom remained with him during his wayward years. An extraordinary truth. Solomon operated in full knowledge; indeed, wisdom explains the truth and power of his explanations.

> **Ecclesiastes 2:9** *So I was great, and increased more than all that were before me in Jerusalem:* ***also my wisdom remained with me.***

Always, wisdom and knowledge is a two edge sword, for those walking with the Lord and for backsliders. God instructs Christians to seek wisdom, yet it comes with a price. Christians prayerfully should ponder, how much they really want to know? God promises a consequence of wisdom is grief and with knowledge comes sorrow.

> **Proverbs 4:7** *Wisdom is the principal thing; therefore get wisdom: and with all thy getting get understanding.*

> **Proverbs 8:11** *For wisdom is better than rubies; and all the things that may be desired are not to be compared to it.*

Ecclesiastes 1:18 For in much wisdom is much grief: and he that increaseth knowledge increaseth sorrow.

Ecclesiastes 7:3 Sorrow is better than laughter: for by the sadness of the countenance the heart is made better.

THE LOGIC BEHIND BACKSLIDING

Ecclesiastes 6:1-2 There is an evil which I have seen under the sun, and it is common among men: 2 A man to whom God hath given riches, wealth, and honour, so that he wanteth nothing for his soul of all that he desireth, yet God giveth him not power to eat thereof, but a stranger eateth it: this is vanity, and it is an evil disease.

The evil disease to which Solomon refers describes dissatisfaction and the inability to enjoy life. No backslider enjoys life; therefore all backsliders suffer this evil disease. Solomon likens the contentment a hungry person enjoys after eating a meal to being content in life. Imagine being extremely hungry, sitting down and eating a delicious meal, yet never feeling full. That is exactly how people feel who attempt to satisfy their spiritual needs with materialism and worldly possessions. They may seem to have everything, but they just can't enjoy it. Everything deceives them. There is always something that stops them. And then adding to their misery, they perceive other people enjoy what they cannot enjoy.

Solomon grew bored and angry with life. This happens to Christians who try to supplement (if not replace) their relationship with God with worldly pleasures. So many people want more from this world than it can possibly deliver, especially in cultures demanding satisfaction and entertainment constantly. Satan creates a world for people to desire that does not exist, portrayed on television, tablets, internet, and movies. Reality actually becomes undesirable. Christians want the world's satisfaction, but God created them for heaven. Be not deceived, sinful behaviors satisfy lost people far more than they satisfy Christians. If you belong to God, sin will not thrill you like it used to do.

Everything is overrated, even for unbelievers; nothing delivers like one hopes or expects. Trying to get satisfaction apart from God always leaves one unsatisfied. Knowing all this, Solomon still partook of the lusts of the flesh as much as was humanly possible. Sadly, more than a few Christians do the same. King Solomon explored every avenue a human being could travel. He found it all a vexation and a deception. And that is exactly what backsliding does for Christians; it makes them miserable. There is just minimal fulfillment to keep a backslider desiring for more. Rather like gambling or the lottery, every now and then the illusion of winning, but overall vanity and deception.

Ecclesiastes 2:1-12 I said in mine heart, Go to now, I will prove thee with mirth, therefore enjoy pleasure: and, behold, this also is vanity. 2 I said of laughter, It is mad: and of mirth, What doeth it? 3 I sought in mine heart to give myself unto wine, yet acquainting mine heart with wisdom; and to lay hold on folly, till I might see what was that good for the sons of men, which they should do under the heaven all the days of their life. 4 I made me great works; I builded me houses; I planted me vineyards: 5 I made me gardens and orchards, and I planted trees in them of all kind of fruits: 6 I made me pools of water, to water therewith the wood that bringeth forth trees: 7 I got me servants and maidens, and had servants born in my house; also I had great possessions of great and small cattle above all that were in Jerusalem before me: 8 I gathered me also silver and gold, and the peculiar treasure of kings and of the provinces: I gat me men singers and women singers, and the delights of the sons of men, as musical instruments, and that of all sorts. 9 So I was great, and increased more than all that were before me in

*Jerusalem: also my wisdom remained with me. **10** And whatsoever mine eyes desired I kept not from them, I withheld not my heart from any joy; for my heart rejoiced in all my labour: and this was my portion of all my labour. **11** Then I looked on all the works that my hands had wrought, and on the labour that I had laboured to do: and, behold, all was vanity and vexation of spirit, and there was no profit under the sun. **12** And I turned myself to behold wisdom, and madness, and folly: for what can the man do that cometh after the king? even that which hath been already done.*

Finally, a cruel trap is set for those who pursue evil. Simply because people seem to get away with sin, meaning God does not judge immediately; people continue to act in unrighteous ways. Backsliders often deceive themselves by interpreting God's inaction as an endorsement, or at least an allowance, of their misbehavior. Rationalizing statements like: *God does not care all that much about... or this sin is really not that big of deal...etc.* are perhaps the biggest vanities and deceptions. Continued backsliding results in judgment. And judgment can be devastating. Ultimately unrepentant sin can cost eternal losses for a Christian's inheritance. (See Judgment Seat of Christ)

The wisest man lived much of his life in backslidden misery. I believe Solomon repented from his sins and wrote Ecclesiastes shortly before he died. The man who had everything summarized living in the last verses of his book. Apostle Paul warns Christians in much the same manner

*Ecclesiastes 12:13-14 Let us hear the conclusion of the whole matter: Fear God, and keep his commandments: for this is the whole duty of man. **14** For God shall bring every work into judgment, with every secret thing, whether it be good, or whether it be evil.*

*Colossians 3:24-25 Knowing that of the Lord ye shall receive the reward of the inheritance: for ye serve the Lord Christ. **25** But he*

that doeth wrong shall receive for the wrong which he hath done: and there is no respect of persons.

Thought to ponder:
Under the reign of Solomon, the nation Israel reached her zenith in righteousness and peace. Solomon led the Lord's people to world power status. He actually represented a type of Jesus' ruling in the Millennium. But after scripture declares 666 talents of gold come to him in one year, King Solomon takes his dark turn and becomes a type of the Antichrist.

1 Kings 10:14 Now the weight of gold that came to Solomon in one year was six hundred threescore and six talents of gold,

Chapter Notes

Ecclesiastes 8:11 Because sentence against an evil work is not executed speedily, therefore the heart of the sons of men is fully set in them to do evil.

Galatians 6:7 Be not deceived; God is not mocked: for whatsoever a man soweth, that shall he also reap.

1 Corinthians 5:5 To deliver such an one unto Satan for the destruction of the flesh, that the spirit may be saved in the day of the Lord Jesus.

2 Corinthians 5:10 For we must all appear before the judgment seat of Christ; that every one may receive the things done in his body, according to that he hath done, whether it be good or bad.

1 Corinthians 3:15 *If any man's work shall be burned, he shall suffer loss: but he himself shall be saved; yet so as by fire.*

Ecclesiastes 5:7 For in the multitude of dreams and many words *there are* also *divers* vanities: but fear thou God.

Ps 19:12 *Who can understand his errors? cleanse thou me from secret faults.*

Ephesians 4:30 *And grieve not the holy Spirit of God, whereby ye are sealed unto the day of redemption*

Ephesians 4:22 *That ye put off concerning the former conversation the old man, which is corrupt according to the deceitful lusts;* **23** *And be renewed in the spirit of your mind;* **24** *And that ye put on the new man, which after God is created in righteousness and true holiness.* **25** *Wherefore putting away lying, speak every man truth with his neighbour: for we are members one of another.* **26** *Be ye angry, and sin not: let not the sun go down upon your wrath:* **27** *Neither give place to the devil.* **28** *Let him that stole steal no more: but rather let him labour, working with his hands the thing which is good, that he may have to give to him that needeth.* **29** *Let no corrupt communication proceed out of your mouth, but that which is good to the use of edifying, that it may minister grace unto the hearers.* **30** *And grieve not the holy Spirit of God, whereby ye are sealed unto the day of redemption.* **31** *Let all bitterness, and wrath, and anger, and clamour, and evil speaking, be put away from you, with all malice:* **32** *And be ye kind one to another, tenderhearted, forgiving one another, even as God for Christ's sake hath forgiven you.*

The Enemy

§

Allegorical Instruction for Hunters and Shooters

Ephesians 6:13-17 Wherefore take unto you the whole armour of God, that ye may be able to withstand in the evil day, and having done all, to stand. 14 Stand therefore, having your loins girt about with truth, and having on the breastplate of righteousness; 15 And your feet shod with the preparation of the gospel of peace; 16 Above all, taking the shield of faith, wherewith ye shall be able to quench all the fiery darts of the wicked. 17 And take the helmet of salvation, and the sword of the Spirit, which is the word of God:

"Now don't start fussing with that car tonight!" said Eleanor. Winston Copperstone stopped buffing his 1965 Ford Mustang and looked toward the open garage door. His wife stood in the driveway. The setting sun glowed behind her, and when she moved streaks of light hit him in the eyes. "Tomorrow is the seventh day," she said.

"I know," said Winston. "I won't be long."

"You need your sleep. A man can't fight if he's tired."

"I'll be right in," said Winston. Turning around, he looked at his suit of armour hanging on the wall. He touched the welded plate covering the left breast and shuddered, remembering all too clearly the lost battle and the spear that pierced the steel.

Inside the house, he took off his shoes and dirty sweatshirt in the laundry room, and then he headed upstairs for a shower.

"Would you like me to load your rifle?" asked Eleanor.

Winston stuck his soapy head outside the shower curtain. "Thanks baby, but I feel better if I do that myself."

"Okay," said Eleanor. "How come you took the scope off?"

"This time I'm going to wait until he gets close. Maybe then he'll go down."

"Oh," she said. "That sounds like a good idea. I'm going to set your armour in the den so it won't be cold in the morning when you put it on."

"I love you," said Winston, and he puckered his lips.

"Oh, rinse off and come to bed," said Eleanor, and she slammed the bathroom door.

The alarm clock announced the seventh day with an electrical buzzing noise. Winston stumbled across the room and dropped his hand on a glowing box of numbers. Feeling afraid, he stood still for a while in the quiet and the dark. He knelt at the bedside and mumbled a few sentences. Eleanor held his hand and said amen when he finished. Winston kissed her forehead even though she had fallen back to sleep.

After a quick shower and a cup of black coffee, he dressed and went into the den. Eleanor left his gun on the couch. He loaded it slowly, pausing between each of the five bullets. Then he put on his armour and slung the rifle over his shoulder.

Dawn was waiting when he opened the front door. The sun, looking like an orange ball emerging from a gray sea, illuminated the mist floating over his lawn. He trudged across the grass and down the street to the meadow. Somewhere in the distance a whip-poor-will called; it seemed to say "Run away, run away."

Where the street ended, an embankment rose up like a great wall. He climbed the slope and stood on top looking across the valley. Below him, a horse waited dressed in full battle armour. Winston sat on the grass and slid down the hill as a child might descend a carpeted stairway.

Awkwardly, he climbed into the saddle. He rode slowly, listening for the enemy. Soon he saw a knight on horseback trotting towards him. Winston caused his horse to veer left. The oncoming rider stayed with him. Turning abruptly, Winston stopped his horse and pulled the bolt back on his rifle.

"Come on you ugly tin can," said Winston. "I got 30-.06 surprise for you this morning."

The enemy leveled his lance and charged. Winston waited until he was about 75 yards away before firing. The knight took two direct hits in the chest, but he kept coming, his lance steady and pointed right at Winston's heart. A split second before impact, Winston let go a third round hitting the enemy in the neck. It didn't stop him, and the long spear slammed into Winston's breastplate.

Winston lay flat on his back choking. He tore off his helmet, and gasped painfully for air. His chest felt as if he'd been hit with a sledge hammer. Unbelievably, he still held the rifle. Staggering to his feet, he faced the enemy.

"Show your face coward," whispered Winston. "Show your face and I'll blow your head off."

The knight sat motionless in his saddle. Winston felt him staring from behind the steel mask. The enemy seemed to know everything about him, to anticipate his next move. Winston rammed a fourth cartridge into the chamber. He sighted in the enemy's head. Then he changed his mind; he dropped his aim and fired. The horse went down, and the enemy toppled forward into the wet grass.

"Ha, ha, so you're not so invincible after all. So much for your regular seventh day victory battle against Winston Copperstone, I don't know why I didn't think of shooting your horse before."

The knight rose to his feet and walked over to Winston. He ripped the rifle from Winston's hands and started beating him with the stock. Large dents appeared all over Winston's armour. At last the rifle broke in half. Winston lay on the ground moaning. He felt wet and slippery inside the armour. Apparently satisfied, his enemy walked over to Winston's horse. Barely conscious, Winston watched him ride away across the meadow. After about an hour, Winston staggered to his feet and hobbled home.

"The day after the seventh day is the first day," said the Preacher. "So has it been since the beginning."

The Copperstones sat in the midst of four hundred people. Disinterested, for the moment, Winston looked around at the congregation. Most the men displayed bruises on their faces; many walked into the auditorium using crutches. The women didn't look as bad, but women cover things with make-up. Even the Preacher had a band aid over his right eye. And when he wiped his forehead, Winston noticed white gauze encircled his hand. After the Preacher stopped talking, Winston and his wife went home and took a nap.

The next morning, Winston still felt sore and tired, but he went to work anyway. Winston Copperstone owned a small grocery store. And he worked very hard five days a week. A delivery truck was waiting in the parking lot.

"That's odd," thought Winston. "I'm not expecting any deliveries until Wednesday."

The truck driver hurried over as soon as Winston parked his car.

"Hello, Harry," said Winston recognizing the driver.

"Mr. Copperstone, I got a deal I think you might be interested in."

"What's that?" asked Winston.

"I got a whole steer, weighs over five hundred pounds." Harry looked around nervously and moved closer to Winston. "You can have it for two fifty. But you gotta pay me cash, and keep no record of the delivery."

Winston took a deep breath and scratched his chin. "Two hundred," he said.

"You'll clear a thousand bucks, Mr. Copperstone," said Harry.

"Take it or leave it," said Winston, and he started walking towards the store.

"I'll take it," said Harry.

Without turning around, Winston smiled and said, "I'll meet you around back."

Three hours later, Winston had the cow butchered and ready for sale. Putting a tray of steaks in the display cooler, his arms and hands ached and were covered with blood. The door chime rang announcing a customer. Robert Darrow, a man from Winston's church, walked in and stood in front of the meat counter.

"Hello Winston."

"Hi Rob, what can I do for you?"

"That's the best price on porterhouse I've seen in years," said Robert. "I'll take four of them."

"Coming right up," said Winston, as he washed the blood off his arms, in the sink. When Winston reached for the steaks, Robert noticed the blood and bruises on his friend's hands.

"Those bruises look terrible, brother."

"Yeah, the enemy beat me up pretty bad yesterday," said Winston. "You, on the other hand look like you didn't even get a scratch. What's the deal, you quit fighting?"

"No, I was on the battlefield, but lately I've been holding my own."

"What are you using on him, a tank?"

"Actually, I'm using an entirely different approach these days. It's not the gun that gets him," said Robert. "It's talking with God and reading the Bible."

"Hey, I pray before I go, it doesn't help."

"Not just on the seventh day," said Robert, "I mean talking with God all the time. Like when you're driving to work, or raking the leaves, or waxing that car of yours."

"Robert, my enemy could care less if I pray! I'm talking about the tin woodsman from Hell! I've never even seen his face."

"That's your problem," said Robert. "Once I saw my enemy's face, I started to hurt him, and hurt him good."

"How'd you get the shield off his face?"

"I already told you," said Robert. "Then one day I hit him, and it just fell off."

"Fell off!? I don't know what kind of enemy you fight, but he sure isn't anything like mine. He almost killed me with that blasted lance of his. Tore right through my armour, and I had to have it welded. He beat me senseless with my own rifle. Then the creep stole my horse. But you know what, Rob?"

"What?" said Robert?

"I shot his horse and killed it. That proves to me I can get him with fire power."

"Winston, you're not at war with his horse, you're at war with him."

"I'm thinking seriously of buying a .460 Weatherby," said Winston. "Only problem it kicks so hard, I don't think I could shoot it more than once from my saddle."

"Why worry about that?" said Robert sarcastically. "He's got your horse anyway."

"Hey! You're right. I can handle five shots from the ground, especially if I brace the gun on a bipod."

Robert shook his head. "You just don't get it, do you?"

"Need anything besides these steaks?" asked Winston already thinking about the new rifle he was going to buy.

"No thank you," said Robert.

The rest of the week went fast. Winston bought a Weatherby Mark V Rifle on Tuesday, and he got to practice at the range on Wednesday. Nothing else important happened until Thursday when Laurie Quilber came into the store. She wanted mint chocolate chip ice-cream, and said she couldn't find it. Winston watched her several moments before walking over to the freezer. Laurie leaned into Winston's hip as he rummaged through the freezer. And Winston put his hand on the lady's lower side reaching for the carton.

"Here it is," said Winston, and he handed her the ice-cream.

"Thank you," she said.

"Will that be all?" asked Winston. He hesitated before walking back behind the counter.

"I guess," she said with a wink, "for today anyway."

On the morning of the seventh day, Winston rose earlier than usual. He packed a shovel, three gallons of gasoline, a rag, one glass bottle, and his new rifle into a wheelbarrow. He reached the battle-field it was still dark. Using his shovel, he dug a shallow, rectangular hole in the ground. The morning air was cold, but Winston per-spired heavily inside his armour. Next, he filled the bottle with gaso-line, stuffed the rag in its top, and set it in the wheelbarrow. Then he mounded up some dirt for the rifle's bipod about twenty feet in front of the hole. So confident his plan would work, he removed his helmet and tossed it on the grass. "The tin can man is in big trouble today!"

Hearing the snorting of a horse, Winston looked across the bat-tle field, straining to see through dawn's gray light. Sure enough, his enemy galloped toward him, slightly to his left, and on Winston's horse too.

"Hey! Tin Can Man," he yelled, "I'm over here." Winston lay in front of the hole with his rifle ready.

The enemy turned and came straight towards him.

BOOM, the crack of a high powered rifle broke the morning's quiet.

"Ha! Ha! I told you no more charges in this war!"

His enemy pulled himself from beneath the horse and continued on foot.

Winston poured the remaining gasoline into the hole, and then ran back to his gun. The knight was heading right for him. Winston held his breath and hoped he didn't smell the gas. When the enemy walked through the shallow hole, Winston pulled the trigger. The blast knocked the night backward into the hole.

With a butane lighter, Winston lit the rag in the bottle. "I'm not sure you drink," he yelled, "but I mixed this cocktail real special!" He threw the bottle, and his enemy disappeared behind a wall of flame.

After a few seconds, the enemy emerged, his whole body sheeted in fire. Winston shot twice knocking him back into the hole. Then he lifted his rifle, and ran towards the blaze. Winston could see his enemy sprawled across the ground. He fired the last round, and the knight's head snapped from the bullet hitting his helmet.

"There," yelled Winston, "that should take care of..." Incredibly, his enemy was up and coming towards him. In desperation, Winston threw his rifle. The knight brushed the gun aside and grabbed Winston's wrists. Pulling him close, he pressed Winston's hands against his armour. Bare flesh meeting hot steel sizzled like bacon. Winston screamed, his face inches from a red hot mask. He could feel his enemy's eyes; somehow he could see from behind the glowing steel. The vile devil sensed his every move. Winston spit; the saliva boiled into steam. Pulling and turning his head sideways did not break the precarious embrace, nor did it prevent Winston's enemy from pressing Winston's face against his mask.

After church the next day, Robert Darrow visited Winston in the burn center at the big university hospital. A nurse led him to his room at the end of a long hallway. Eleanor sat in a chair beside Winston's bed. Her hair was a mess, and she had obviously been crying.

"You look like a mummy," said Robert walking into the room.

"It's not as bad as it looks," said Winston speaking through a hole in the bandages. Holes had also been cut so he could see. "My hands and one side of my face got burned badly, but the rest of me is all right."

"From what I heard," said Robert, "It's lucky you didn't get killed! You're going to wear the scars for the rest of your life."

"Yeah, I guess I'm going about this fight all wrong," said Winston. "I'm going to follow your advice."

"That's good news," said Robert glancing at an open Bible lying next to the bed. "Prayer and Scripture are the only things that hurt your enemy."

"So how'd you do yesterday, Rob?"

Robert held up his index finger, a small band aid wrapped around the tip. "He got me some, but I stuck him with the sword and that sent him running."

Winston looked enviously at Robert's finger. A nurse entered the room with a hypodermic syringe in her hand. "Visiting hour is over for Mr. Copperstone," she said. "Mrs. Copperstone, you can stay but the gentleman has to leave."

"Eleanor," said Winston. "You go home and get some sleep. I need to spend some time alone. There's someone I've got to talk with."

Two months later, Winston felt ready to fight again. He rose early on the seventh day, and went into the den to pray. Putting on his breastplate, he noticed the welded plate over the left breast was gone, the steel smooth as if it was never punctured. The dents also, had disappeared. His helmet fit securely, with no uncomfortable rubbing against the scars on his face.

Winston decided on the weapon that came with the armour, a weapon he had not yet proved. The two edged sword seemed like a toy compared to his arsenal of high powered rifles, but now, as he held it in his hand, he felt more confident than ever. Finally, he went to the garage and took the shield down from its lonely perch beside the Mustang. A reddish cloud of dust floated onto the car. Fully pre- pared for battle, Winston walked bravely to the meadow.

Mounted atop a huge black stallion, the enemy waited. He held a long and sturdy lance. Winston knelt for a moment, and then ran to meet him. The enemy charged with fierce anger, holding the lance downward in order to strike his opponent. Winston stopped; he held the shield before him and braced for the collision. The impact knocked him several yards backward, and he felt tremendous pain in his wrist. But the shield held. The awful lance snapped in two. The enemy, himself, thrown from the saddle and lay upon the ground. Winston walked over to the fallen knight and placed a foot on his chest. With the point of his sword, he flipped the helmet from his enemy's head.

Winston gasped and retreated several steps. At last he knew the enemy who sought him so much hurt. Finally, he met the hellish foe, the great destroyer, the one who mocked Jesus' grace over and over and over again. For there, on the battle field, stretching from salvation to heaven, Winston Copperstone stared into the face of himself.

Proverbs 14:14 *The backslider in heart shall be filled with his own ways: and a good man shall be satisfied from himself.*

Romans 6:6 *Knowing this, that our old man is crucified with him, that the body of sin might be destroyed, that henceforth we should not serve sin.*

End

Age of Accountability

§

Romans 4:8 Blessed is the man to whom the Lord will not impute sin.

HAVE YOU EVER CONSIDERED ADAM and Eve lived in the exact opposite spiritual condition as people today? Adam and Eve made a choice in order to lose salvation; while today, people make a choice in order to obtain salvation.

When Adam and Eve disobeyed God and ate from the tree of knowledge of good and evil they died spiritually. From that day forward, human beings are born with a body, soul, and a dead spirit. Our physical birth also includes an inherited Adamic (sinful) nature. That's why Jesus said we must be born again. One way of looking at it is we need to restore what Adam lost.

John 3:3 Jesus answered and said unto him, Verily, verily, I say unto thee, Except a man be born again, he cannot see the kingdom of God.

Does John 3:3 mean all people, without exception, must be born again in order to go to heaven? Let's suppose a one-year-old child dies. Does the child go to heaven? What about the mentally impaired person? Does Jesus impart salvation to some persons who did not consciously believe in him?

Thinking about these kinds of situations necessitates the concept of an age of accountability. An age of accountability constitutes theological theory that God does not hold children accountable for their sin. In other words- God lets them into heaven without being born again. Nearly all Christians agree with this idea, but there is little agreement on a set chronological age for when a person becomes accountable. This topic makes Christians nervous even to talk about, let alone, ask challenging questions. But troubling or not, this is a very serious matter and necessitates serious study.

An age of accountability makes Christians uncomfortable because, ultimately, it means God allows some people into heaven without being born again. Or perhaps more accurately- some people get to heaven without trusting Christ in the same way a lost, repentant sinner is able to do? As long as exceptions to the salvation rule stay simple there is not too much anguish: Children, aborted babies, mentally disabled persons, etc. But when examples include teenagers who die from drugs, car accidents, suicides, or even natural causes, Christians feel less confident about what they believe. Even the world's stereotypical questions, remain uncomfortably unanswered. Questions like, what about primitive peoples living in some foreign land who never heard about Jesus, do they go to hell? What about people in a strict Islamic culture where Christianity is against the law? The Bible answers these questions, but they require some deeper thinking and study.

Ecclesiastes 7:24 *That which is far off, and exceeding deep, who can find it out?*

Before dealing with these questions directly, let's establish an age of accountability exists. An age of accountability is not just some theological theory to help us through tough situations. It is an established biblical fact. God is reasonable. Without racing ahead to prove a chronological age based on emotion or some unfounded religious idea, the first step toward understanding compares scripture with scripture. In the end, however, regardless of a person's age, God decides who is accountable.

Knowledge of good and evil

A profound connection exists between the knowledge of good and evil, and God holding a person responsible for sin. God does not hold people accountable for sin whom he determines *without knowledge of good and evil*.

The theme *knowledge of good and evil* is in the Bible only three times. Examining these passages are essential. God's first reference to the knowledge of good and evil concerns the creation of the tree in the Garden of Eden. The second mention is when God commands Adam and Eve not to eat from that same tree. The third time God brings the topic to discussion, he exempts an entire generation from judgment, 2,500 years later.

> *Genesis 2:9 And out of the ground made the LORD God to grow every tree that is pleasant to the sight, and good for food; the tree of life also in the midst of the garden, and the tree of knowledge of good and evil.*

> *Genesis 2:16-17 And the LORD God commanded the man, saying, Of every tree of the garden thou mayest freely eat: 17 But of the tree of the knowledge of good and evil, thou shalt not eat of it: for in the day that thou eatest thereof thou shalt surely die.*

> *Deuteronomy 1:39 Moreover your little ones, which ye said should be a prey, and your children, which in that day had no knowledge between good and evil, they shall go in thither, and unto them will I give it, and they shall possess it.*

A consequence from eating from the forbidden tree resulted in the acquisition of knowledge of good and evil. Once people acquired this knowledge, God held them accountable. Before they acquired this knowledge God considered them innocent. (Hence the origin of the saying, ignorance is bliss.)

In the book of Deuteronomy, nearly 2,500 years after the Fall- the words *knowledge between good and evil* appear again. God judges Israel according to their knowledge of good and evil. The reader should ponder events recorded in Numbers chapters 13-15. Additional information is discussed in Deuteronomy.

Historical Summary

The Lord recently delivered the Jews from oppressive slavery in Egypt. After spending a little more than one year in the wilderness, Moses sends twelve men to spy out the Promised Land. When those men return, only Joshua and Caleb offer a positive view, and encourage Israel to possess the land. The other ten spies warn about giants and convince Israel the people beyond the Jordan are too powerful to defeat in battle. Their negative report discourages the entire nation, and they refuse to possess the land. In their fear and disobedience, Israel argues their children would be prey, and they should return to Egypt. Israel's refusal to possess the Promised Land infuriates the Lord, and he passes judgment on the entire nation. *Numbers 13:1-2; 30-33*

God's specific judgment merits a Christian's utmost scrutiny. Even though judgement passed on the entire nation, God did not hold people under twenty years old responsible. God declares the young people had *no knowledge between good and evil*, therefore, the Lord does not impute sin. Only Persons twenty years old and above were held accountable.

God passes judgment but exempts children because they had no knowledge between good and evil. Think about what the

Lord is doing. A twenty year old and a nineteen year old both murmur against Moses and refuse to do what God says. When judgment
falls, only the twenty year old is held responsible for his sin. Sin is
not imputed to any Israelite under twenty! God draws a clear line; in
this particular instance, twenty years old is the age of accountability.
As we shall see, this is not the only time twenty years old is the des-
ignated age for maturity and responsibility.

*Numbers 14:2-4 And all the children of Israel murmured
against Moses and against Aaron: and the whole congregation said
unto them, Would God that we had died in the land of Egypt! or
would God we had died in this wilderness! 3 And wherefore hath
the LORD brought us unto this land, to fall by the sword, that our
wives and our children should be a prey? were it not better for us to
return into Egypt? 4 And they said one to another, Let us make a
captain, and let us return into Egypt.*

*Numbers 14:27-35 How long shall I bear with this evil congrega-
tion, which murmur against me? I have heard the murmurings of
the children of Israel, which they murmur against me. 28 Say unto
them, As truly as I live, saith the LORD, as ye have spoken in mine
ears, so will I do to you: 29 Your carcases shall fall in this wilderness;
and all that were numbered of you, according to your whole number,* **from twenty years old and upward, which have murmured against me,** *30 Doubtless ye shall not come into the land,
concerning which I sware to make you dwell therein, save Caleb the
son of Jephunneh, and Joshua the son of Nun.* **31 But your little
ones, which ye said should be a prey, them will I bring in,
and they shall know the land which ye have despised.** *32 But
as for you, your carcases, they shall fall in this wilderness. 33 And
your children shall wander in the wilderness forty years, and bear
your whoredoms, until your carcases be wasted in the wilderness.
34 After the number of the days in which ye searched the land,*

even forty days, each day for a year, shall ye bear your iniquities, even forty years, and ye shall know my breach of promise. 35 I the LORD have said, I will surely do it unto all this evil congregation, that are gathered together against me: in this wilderness they shall be consumed, and there they shall die.

Numbers 32:11 *Surely none of the men that came up out of Egypt, from twenty years old and upward, shall see the land which I sware unto Abraham, unto Isaac, and unto Jacob; because they have not wholly followed me:*

Deuteronomy 1:39 *Moreover your little ones, which ye said should be a prey, and your children, which in that day had no knowledge between good and evil, they shall go in thither, and unto them will I give it, and they shall possess*

TWENTY YEARS OLD; AN ESTABLISHED AGE OF ACCOUNTABILITY

Even before Israel refused to take the Promised Land, God established twenty years old with accountability. In the passage below God teaches a critical doctrine. It is not the money that's important; God values all souls equally. But God exempts children under twenty years from requiring a ransom or payment. Israelites under twenty do not make an offering; teenagers did not have to make atonement for their souls.

Over and over again, the Bible gives the chronological age of responsibility is twenty. At twenty years old God considers people responsible for their actions. When it came to counting people for war, for service in the priesthood, or for taking a census, the age of twenty is consistent.

Perhaps we should not conclude twenty as the absolute chronological threshold, but it certainly was an important legal age set by

God. Most significantly, I think the most important point here is God recognizes a difference between youth and maturity. When it comes to entering heaven or hell- God is the judge of the matter. Who possess the knowledge between good and evil is God's decision, not religious leadership.

CONSIDER:

Exodus 30:11-15 And the LORD spake unto Moses, saying, 12 When thou takest the sum of the children of Israel after their number, **then shall they give every man a ransom for his soul unto the LORD,** *when thou numberest them; that there be no plague among them, when thou numberest them. 13 This they shall give, every one that passeth among them that are numbered, half a shekel after the shekel of the sanctuary: (a shekel is twenty gerahs:) an half shekel shall be the offering of the LORD.* **14 Every one that passeth among them that are numbered, from twenty years old and above, shall give an offering unto the LORD. 15** *The rich shall not give more, and the poor shall not give less than half a shekel, when they give an offering unto the LORD, to make an atonement for your souls.*

Numbers 1:2-3 Take ye the sum of all the congregation of the children of Israel, after their families, by the house of their fathers, with the number of their names, every male by their polls; **3 From twenty years old and upward,** *all that are able to go forth to war in Israel: thou and Aaron shall number them by their armies.*

Numbers 1:18 And they assembled all the congregation together on the first day of the second month, and they declared their pedigrees after their families, by the house of their fathers, according to the number of the names, **from twenty years old and upward, by their polls.**

Numbers 26:1-2 *And it came to pass after the plague, that the LORD spake unto Moses and unto Eleazar the son of Aaron the priest, saying, 2 Take the sum of all the congregation of the children of Israel,* ***from twenty years old and upward****, throughout their fathers' house, all that are able to go to war in Israel.*

Numbers 32:11 *Surely none of the men that came up out of Egypt, from* ***twenty years old and upward****, shall see the land which I sware unto Abraham, unto Isaac, and unto Jacob; because they have not wholly followed me:*

1 Chronicles 23:24 *These were the sons of Levi after the house of their fathers; even the chief of the fathers, as they were counted by number of names by their polls, that did the work for the service of the house of the LORD,* ***from the age of twenty years and upward.***

Ezra 3:8 *Now in the second year of their coming unto the house of God at Jerusalem, in the second month, began Zerubbabel the son of Shealtiel, and Jeshua the son of Jozadak, and the remnant of their brethren the priests and the Levites, and all they that were come out of the captivity unto Jerusalem; and appointed the Levites,* ***from twenty years old and upward, to set forward the work of the house*** *of the LORD.*

GUILT AND KNOWLEDGE

Consider people who absolutely go to hell. Examining scriptures discussing the damned, also sheds light on accountability. Observe every time the Lord discusses people going to hell, he tells us, in one way or another, that they have knowledge of good and evil.

In Romans chapter one, God discusses a group of people who *hold the truth in unrighteousness.* These people know the truth; they are not ignorant. God draws them to himself and convinced them the gospel truth, yet they choose to remain in their sins. They reject the Lord's mercy. God continues his justification for their damnation by declaring they knew the truth, and even possessed knowledge of God. Their darkened hearts and eventual damnation was a consequence of their own choices. To reject God, one must be offered God. No ignorant persons exist in Romans chapter one.

> ***Romans 1:18-21*** *For the wrath of God is revealed from heaven against all ungodliness and unrighteousness of men,* ***who hold the truth in unrighteousness;*** *19 Because that which may be known of God is manifest in them; for* ***God hath shewed it unto them.*** *20 For the invisible things of him from the creation of the world are clearly seen, being understood by the things that are made, even his eternal power and Godhead; so that* ***they are without excuse:*** *21 Because that,* ***when they knew God, they glorified him not as God, neither were thankful;*** *but became vain in their imaginations, and their foolish heart was darkened.*

Jesus speaks to another group of salvation rejecters in the Gospel of John. Astoundingly, Jesus actually declares if he hadn't spoken to them, they would not have sin! But because they heard with their ears and saw with their eyes, they were without excuse. They became guilty after God revealed to them the truth. Just like Christ rejecters in New Testament times, people who go to hell today -absolutely choose to stay lost.

> ***John 15:22-24*** *If I had not come and spoken unto them, they had not had sin: but now they have no cloke for their sin. 23 He that hateth me hateth my Father also. 24 If I had not done among them the works which none other man did, they had not had sin: but now have they both seen and hated both me and my Father.*

Apostle Paul reveals damned persons living in our own age also know about Jesus, but choose to reject him. Observe *they received not the love of the truth*. This means they were offered the truth and refused it. They also *believed not the truth*. In order to not believe something, one has to know about it. There is no ignorance here.

> *2 Thessalonians 2:10-12 And with all deceivableness of unrighteousness in them that perish; because **they received not the love of the truth**, that they might be saved. **11** And for this cause God shall send them strong delusion, that they should believe a lie: **12** That they all might be damned **who believed not the truth**, but had pleasure in unrighteousness.*

Again, God draws them to himself, and through the witness of the Holy Ghost, he reveals their lost condition. But they loved their own sins and said no to Jesus Christ. God deluding their minds and causing them to believe a lie was done after they rejected God. In order to *obey not the gospel*, one hears and comprehends the gospel and then chooses to reject it. There is no ignorance here.

> *2 Thessalonians 1:7-9 And to you who are troubled rest with us, when the Lord Jesus shall be revealed from heaven with his mighty angels, **8** In flaming fire taking vengeance on them that know not God, and **that obey not the gospel of our Lord Jesus** Christ: **9** Who shall be punished with everlasting destruction from the presence of the Lord, and from the glory of his power;*

CONCLUSION

Scriptural evidence proves God discriminates between young people and adults. Old Testament Scripture declared God did not hold teenagers responsible for sin like he did for people over twenty years old. Some Christians teach the age of accountability is seven or twelve.

Then offer very weak theories to support what they believe. The reason for these mistakes is Christians believe (in their hearts) God will not send children to hell. Their problem is they don't understand the topic well enough to prove it. So they pick a very young age and hope no one challenges what they say. The end result is many Christians know little more than feelings about an age of accountability.

When people believe in an age of accountability doctrine, they correctly acknowledge a huge gray area exists concerning judgment. Be it a young child, the mentally disabled or primitive heathens in some foreign land- if God has not drawn and convinced them of Jesus Christ, then they would not be judged for rejecting him. If God does not do his supernatural part, it would not matter if you were 2 years old, 17 years old, or a thirty-five year old genius. The whole triune God involves himself in man's salvation: No man comes to Jesus Christ, except the Father draw him. And Jesus reveals the Father. And the Holy Ghost convicts their sin. The reason people go to hell is because they reject Jesus Christ. Scripture declares in no uncertain terms that God must intervene in lost people's hearts and minds in order for salvation to happen. This does not mean God forces a person to choose him, but it certainly means God makes the first move.

John 6:44 No man can come to me, except the Father which hath sent me draw him: and I will raise him up at the last day.

Matthew 11:27 All things are delivered unto me of my Father: and no man knoweth the Son, but the Father; neither knoweth any man the Father, save the Son, and he to whomsoever the Son will reveal him.

John 16:7-8 Nevertheless I tell you the truth; It is expedient for you that I go away: for if I go not away, the Comforter will not come unto you; but if I depart, I will send him unto you. 8 And when he is come, he will reprove the world of sin, and of righteousness, and of judgment: see also John 16:12-15

Psalms 14:2-3 *The LORD looked down from heaven upon the children of men, to see if there were any that did understand, and seek God. 3 They are all gone aside, they are all together become filthy: there is none that doeth good, no, not one.*

Obviously, in this day and age many young people receive God's gift of salvation at a very early age. This does not mean an age of accountability does not exist in the Church Age. It simply means God's grace and faith in Jesus Christ supersedes whenever God moves. Only God knows the hearts and minds of human beings. What people go through, their environment, and their emotional and psychological health are all factors in God's judgment. God is always reasonable. Just as God determined who was held accountable in Joshua's generation, so does God today. God deals with people on an individual basis. Just exactly when an individual reaches his/her age of accountability is determined by God. Christians preach the word of God. We reprove, rebuke, and exhort with all longsuffering and doctrine. It does not weaken the Gospel to point out God's mercy.

Suicide

THROUGHOUT THIS BOOK, WE HAVE seen numerous Bible characters consider taking their own life, several prophets actually asked God to kill them: Moses, Elijah, Jonah to name three. But contemplating suicide and actually doing it are two very different actions. Many Christians deal with consequences from someone's suicide. The tragedy leaves families and friends stunned; even when we know it might be coming.

According the CDC (Centers for Disease Control and Prevention) Suicide was the tenth leading cause of death for all ages in 2013. There were 41,149 suicides in 2013 in the United States—a rate of 12.6 per 100,000 is equal to 113 suicides each day or one every 13 minutes. Males take their own lives at nearly four times the rate of females and represent 77.9% of all suicides

Suicide is the third leading cause of death among persons aged 10-14, the second among persons aged 15-34 years, the fourth among persons aged 35-44 years, the fifth among persons aged 45-54 years, the eighth among person 55-64 years, and the seventeenth among persons 65 years and older.

In 2013, the United States Department of Veterans Affairs released a study that covered suicides from 1999 to 2010, which showed that 22 veterans were committing suicide per day, or one every 65 minutes. More than double the civilian rate.

The reasons why people commit suicide share some common threads; their biggest correlation is pain: be it emotional, psychological, or physical. People taking their own lives want to get out of pain. I believe suicide is predominately a spiritual problem. This does not mean professional medical help should be avoided. I also believe mental illness often plays a role.

Another traumatic consequence of suicide is the manner society reacts, especially the way family and friends respond. With the best intentions people can make things worse. Religious people are among the worst offenders. In fairness, we can also be the most helpful.

The common assertion that suicide is unforgivable has no biblical basis what so ever. Jesus died for sinners and no sin is unforgivable. The idea a Christian cannot commit suicide is also not true. If mental illness is present, a person may be no more responsible for his/her suicide than having cancer or a heart attack.

However, if the reader is considering suicide, there is still judgment, and you will face God. You do not die and end it all, you die and face it all. Anyone thinking about suicide needs to seek help immediately. The very fact you are worried about taking your life, shows you are looking for another choice. Help is out there; find it. If someone is hurting you, report it to legal authorities. Doctor prescribed medications help thousands of people, perhaps you are chemically out of sorts? Read the last chapter in this book.

If ever suicide touches a friend, and you truly don't know what to do, remember Job's friends. The most effective advice they gave Job happened during their first week of visitation. For seven days and seven nights they said nothing. They quietly sat together, joined in empathetic compassion for Job. Sometimes just being there and caring is all friends should do. Although Job did not take his own life, the chapter on *Job* correlates very appropriately with suicide- and suicide prevention.

Job 2: 13 So they sat down with him upon the ground seven days and seven nights, and none spake a word unto him: for they saw that his grief was very great.

Before any meaningful dialog on suicide begins, investigating circumstances surrounding the tragedy is imperative. If a person takes his/her life to avoid horrible persecution like sexual abuse, or even incessant bullying, although technically classified a suicide, the person who dies is the victim of a crime; or at the very least, a moral tragedy for which he/she is not responsible.

Suicide leaves a wake of sorrow. Questions engulf survivors like a dark, anguishing cloud. As Christian comforters let us pray for wisdom and compassion; let not presume knowledge when we do not know. Righteous judgment never omits mercy.

> *John 7:24 Judge not according to the appearance, but judge righteous judgment.*

> *Psalms 31:7 I will be glad and rejoice in thy mercy: for thou hast considered my trouble; thou hast known my soul in adversities;*

The Bible records several suicides:

Abimelech, a judge killed himself after being mortally wounded. He worried about posterity crediting a woman for his demise, thinking a female defeating him in battle was too humiliating. So with death inevitable, and reputation at stake, he ordered a soldier to kill him.

> *Judges 9:52-54 And Abimelech came unto the tower, and fought against it, and went hard unto the door of the tower to burn it with fire. 53 And a certain woman cast a piece of a millstone upon Abimelech's head, and all to brake his skull. 54 Then he called hastily unto the young man his armourbearer, and said unto him, Draw thy sword, and slay me, that men say not of me, A woman slew him. And his young man thrust him through, and he died..*

Samson, after decades of backsliding and serving God intermittently, this famous strong man ends up imprisoned by his enemies.

They blinded him and made his life a spectacle, using him as sport to mock God. Tortured and humiliated, he took his life.

Paradoxically, the New Testament mentions Samson as a faithful believer; not only proving God's mercy, but also reveals God knows things about circumstances unbeknown to all observers. (See chapter *Judgment Seat of Christ* for judgment on Christians' sin)

> *Judges 16:29-30 And Samson took hold of the two middle pillars upon which the house stood, and on which it was borne up, of the one with his right hand, and of the other with his left. 30 And Samson said, Let me die with the Philistines. And he bowed himself with all his might; and the house fell upon the lords, and upon all the people that were therein. So the dead which he slew at his death were more than they which he slew in his life.*

> *Hebrews 11:32-33 And what shall I more say? for the time would fail me to tell of Gedeon, and of Barak, and of Samson, and of Jephthae; of David also, and Samuel, and of the prophets: 33 Who through faith subdued kingdoms, wrought righteousness, obtained promises, stopped the mouths of lions,*

King Saul and his Armourbearer. Both men killed themselves in battle. Mortally wounded and the enemy about to overtake him, King Saul ordered his armourbearer to kill him. Saul feared capture and torture. Such a situation is understandable; it does not depict mental illness.

> *1 Samuel 31:3-5 And the battle went sore against Saul, and the archers hit him; and he was sore wounded of the archers. 4 Then said Saul unto his armourbearer, Draw thy sword, and thrust me through therewith; lest these uncircumcised come and thrust me through, and abuse me. But his armourbearer would not; for he was sore afraid. Therefore Saul took a sword, and fell upon it. 5*

And when his armourbearer saw that Saul was dead, he fell likewise upon his sword, and died with him.

Zimri, an evil king, likewise committed suicide when he saw defeat upon him.

> ***1 Kings 16:18*** *And it came to pass, when Zimri saw that the city was taken, that he went into the palace of the king's house, and burnt the king's house over him with fire, and died,*

Ahithophel, King David's counselor and supposed friend until he sided with Absalom in an attempted overthrow of David. All the people considered Ahithophel a very wise and brilliant counsellor. He enjoyed great respect and reputation. But when people disregarded his advice, and decided to follow another man's counsel, Ahithophel killed himself.

> ***2 Samuel 16:23*** *And the counsel of Ahithophel, which he counselled in those days, was as if a man had inquired at the oracle of God: so was all the counsel of Ahithophel both with David and with Absalom.*

> ***2 Samuel 17:21-23*** *And it came to pass, after they were departed, that they came up out of the well, and went and told king David, and said unto David, Arise, and pass quickly over the water: for thus hath Ahithophel counselled against you.* **22** *Then David arose, and all the people that were with him, and they passed over Jordan: by the morning light there lacked not one of them that was not gone over Jordan.* **23 And when Ahithophel saw that his counsel was not followed, he saddled his ass, and arose, and gat him home to his house, to his city, and put his household in order, and hanged himself, and died, and was buried in the sepulchre of his father.**

At first reading, Ahithophel's suicide seems more pertinent to our study than the battlefield scenarios. Ahithophel suffered psychological and emotional anguish. Mortified at the loss of reputation, he chooses to die. This is pure pride. Suicides like Ahithophel's remind us of those killing themselves over bankruptcy or great embarrassment. Truly he is acting irrational and pathetic.

With a cursory read, these Old Testament suicides may seem rather unrelated to this paper. While unhappiness, loneliness, and depression remain themes in this essay, we can still observe some common threads. In fact, under closer scrutiny, these deaths may indeed teach us truths pertinent to all suicides.

Although Ahithophel's death was not on a battlefield, his country was at war. Thus we observe all the Old Testament suicides took place during time of war. War is ultimately dangerous and unpredictable. People commonly use the word war as a metaphor describing terrible and anguishing situations. Applying a spiritual application to these suicides, I think provides insight and learning.

People contemplating suicide see themselves at war with life. Life is the enemy. An overwhelming enemy advances, their battle is perceived lost. People who kill themselves see their situation as hopeless. These people live under unbearable levels of stress.

TALKING SOMEONE OUT OF SUICIDE

At the time of suicide, self-destroyers are totally self-centered; 100% self-absorbed, thinking only about their own pain. No thoughts of others. No thinking about God or judgment. No thinking about escape.

Being 100% focused on one's self is an observation a counselor can use to turn things around, not to condemn or judge, but to offer hope and alternatives. Try and get a person to think about something other than himself. Talk about the consequences, make him see the ramifications. Get him to realize the people he would hurt. Get the person to realize the self-centeredness of his intended action.

Humiliation, extreme embarrassment, and failure, can and do provoke some persons to consider taking their own life. This kind of hopelessness can be dealt with on a practical level. This kind of pain does not last forever, even though the person suffering thinks it will. Adding to this delusion, pride and self-centeredness communicate a false perception of reality. Make the suffering person see that the world, even close friends, have too many of their own problems to focus very long on anyone else's failure. People are not focused on him as much as he thinks. He can get over it. Life can go on. Recovery is just around the corner. This may seem like brutal therapy, but a potential suicide needs stopped. Once a person starts to think more rationally, healing and compassion continues through caring friends or therapist.

A person humiliated or feeling hopeless, to the point of desiring death, is actually ready for an alternative. And that alternative is Jesus. A Christian counsellor should explain salvation, forgiveness and even repentance. If the counsellor discovers the person is being abused, remove the victim from harm's way, even if legal authorities need advised. But again an alternative to suicide must be offered. If a person is irrationally depressed and in despair- this person may be chemically out of balance; medication could fix the problem. Get the person to a doctor.

Some suicidal situations trace directly to extremely sinful behavior, perhaps even criminal. The person is rational, but does not want to face what's coming next. Such situations require blunt truth: Unrepentant sinners, dying without salvation do not get the relief they seek. Death is no comforter. The fires of hell exist and wait for those who refuse Jesus Christ. Without Jesus as your Saviour, you will die and get just what you deserve. With Jesus as your Saviour you die and go to heaven; it's that simple.

Some crimes the law or society cannot forgive. But Jesus saves and loves those when no one else will. No matter how grievous the sin, Jesus still saves. Personally I know Christians serving life sentences for crimes so heinous, they may even get executed. But after death, heaven waits for them with open gates.

> ***John 3:36*** *He that believeth on the Son hath everlasting life: and he that believeth not the Son shall not see life; but the wrath of God abideth on him.*

> ***John 14:6*** *Jesus saith unto him, I am the way, the truth, and the life: no man cometh unto the Father, but by me.*

Some Things in Life won't Go Away

§

Based on a true story

Psalms 51:3 *For I acknowledge my transgressions: and my sin is ever before me.*

"IN THE DREAM EVERYTHING IS exactly like it was that night," said Mark, "the road, the curve, even the rain comes down the same. After it happens, I pull a woman out of the van, and I can see she's dead. The fire is spreading so I run back to see if anyone else is in the truck. I find this little girl; I grab her and run away from the fire. I'm holding her." Mark stood, his arms positioned as if he were holding a child. "Yeah, I'm holding her, and she opens her eyes, looks right at me! My hands, covered with blood, right beside her face. Then she's gone. I scream and scream but nothing happens, nothing can change the facts."

Dr. Bashik crossed his legs and scribbled some notes on a pad of paper. He had listened to the nightmare many times. He uncrossed his legs and waited for the end.

"Then, everything is different," said Mark, "like I'm watching TV with the volume up real loud, and the channel got switched to a black and white movie with no sound. Now I'm standing in this field of mud staring at my hands. It's raining hard, but the blood won't wash off. A beam of light is shining on my hands. I stick my hands in the mud and rub like crazy, but the blood won't come off."

"Mark," said Dr. Bashik, "it was an accident."

"I was drunk," said Mark, "I murdered them."

"Mark, you served five years in prison, and you haven't had a drink in seven years. You are not a murderer. You are a good man who behaved in an irresponsible manner and had a terrible accident. Forgive yourself."

"I can't. Don't you see? Oh, God, how I wish I died and not them."

"Mark!" Dr. Bashik raised his voice, something he rarely did with patients, "listen to me. Millions of people drive while under the influence of alcohol. They cross the center line and there is no car. They luck out! What happened to you could happen to them. They are as guilty as you."

"God help them," said Mark.

"Mark, you must listen to reason. What you want is to erase that night, to bring those people back to life. And it can't be done. But you cannot continue to live like this."

"There's the answer then," said Mark rising to his feet.

"Sit down," said Dr. Bashik.

"It's no use," said Mark. "You listen to me tell you the same story over and over. And I listen to you tell me the same things. We're kidding ourselves. Some things in life won't go away."

"Where are you going?" asked Dr. Bashik.

"For a walk."

"Will I see you in two weeks?" asked the doctor following him into the hall.

"What for?" said Mark. "Want to hear my dream again?"

"If you need to talk before your next appointment, call me."

"Sure," said Mark walking away, "sure."

Mark drove to his apartment and went inside. He typed a fast note and read it on the monitor. "I'll make it letter quality," he thought.

When the printer stopped, he yanked the paper out and laid it across the keyboard. Without turning off his computer or locking the door, he left.

On his way to the ocean, he stopped at a liquor store and bought a fifth of whiskey. When he got into town, he parked his car in a grocery store's parking lot. A small blue car drove by and stopped a short distance down the street.

Mark pulled back the brown paper bag exposing the neck of the bottle; it had been seven years. He loosed the cap and listened to the plastic seal snap. The swallow went down hard, and he shook his head squeezing his eyes shut. He sat there about a half hour waiting for the night. Then he left his car and started walking. The driver of the small blue car waited a few minutes and got out of his car.

Mark found an isolated bench and sat down. In the foreground he could hear the carnival-like noise of the boardwalk. He could see the pier, foreboding and huge, stretching over the Atlantic. The whiskey went down easy now feeling like an old friend happy to be remembered. A steady breeze blew in from the sea pressing his shirt against his skin. He set the bottle down and turned away from the wind to light a cigarette. After a smoke, and a long drink of whiskey, he stood and walked toward the water; the end of the pier beckoned him. The caps on the waves, reflecting light from the moon, shone a frothy white. Behind the waves, there was solid blackness as if a giant curtain had been drawn. Mark took his keys and threw them at the dark.

He started walking toward the pier; but stopped. A man stood directly in front of him. "Hello, Mark," he said.

"Who are you?" said Mark.

"Bob," said the man.

The man looked familiar, but he couldn't place him. Mark walked closer.

"Bob Weston."

Mark felt sick. He hadn't seen Weston since the trial, seven years ago.

"When did you start drinking again?"

"Tonight," said Mark, "but it's almost over now."

"I never knew what hate was until you," said Bob. "I was glad you went to prison. I've been keeping track of you all these years?"

Mark didn't answer. He turned around and stared at the ocean.

"When your wife left you, I was happy, glad you lost what you took from me. Two years ago, the day you got out of jail, I took a gun and drove around for hours."

"Why didn't you use it?" said Mark turning around.

"I don't know," said Bob, "I just couldn't."

The two men looked directly into each other.

"About a year ago, something happened to me that took away my hate," said Bob, "it enabled me to live again."

"I'll never forgive myself," said Mark, "never. I wish I died and not your family."

"Forgiving yourself won't help," said Bob. "What you need is to be forgiven."

"Your forgiveness is unimaginable," said Mark.

"Maybe," said Bob, "but it's not my forgiveness you need. I'm talking about God. Nothing else can help you. Your problem is guilt. And there's only one place for guilt; you don't need a doctor, you need Jesus Christ."

"I just want to die," said Mark.

"Trouble is," said Bob, "you don't die and end it all, you die and face it all. Did you know the Bible says some men's sins go before them to judgment while other men's sins follow after? No doubt Heaven is aware of you already. And if you die without Jesus Christ, you'll get exactly what you deserve- hell. In a bizarre way, Mark, you have an advantage over other men. Most people think they're pretty good. They have so much pride; they won't admit they're lost."

"Why are you telling me this tonight?" asked Mark.

"The truth is, after I tell you what I came to say, I don't want to ever see you again. But I've known for months God wanted me to tell you. This is as much for me as it is for you. I've been putting it off, but today I knew I had to get it done. Earlier this evening, I drove to your apartment. You were leaving, so I followed you. Now listen close, this is what I came to say. Jesus died for your sin as well as mine. If you let him, he'll take the blame. Come Judgment Day, it will be like he killed my wife and little girl." Tears streamed down Weston's face. "I don't understand how Jesus takes the blame for everyone's sin, but He does." Bob said his last sentence looking at the sky, and then he walked away.

Mark watched him. Wanting to let go of the whiskey, he could not. The alcohol seemed to hit him all at once, and he staggered into the water and fell. The pull from the undertow dragged him out about 20 yards. He reappeared on the surface gasping for air. There was no bottle now. He struggled into shore and crawled up onto the sand. He tried to remember what Bob said about Jesus and forgiveness. Putting it together as best he could, he prayed. Sometime during the prayer, he passed out.

The dream came and everything happened like it had hundreds of times before- until the light beam hit his hands. The blood was gone; his flesh was clean. Then the light moved away leaving him in total blackness. In the distance he could see the light moving through the dark. He ran after the light, wanting to see his hands again. Running blindly, with all his strength, he hit an immovable object. It knocked him to his knees, before him, in full illumination stood an empty cross. Blood ran down the wood and soaked the ground. He crawled forward, desperate to reclaim the guilt he knew belonged to him. Just as he was about to touch the bloodied ground, the vision moved away disappearing in the furthest depths of space.

Psalms 103:12 *As far as the east is from the west, so far hath he removed our transgressions from us.*

Romans 5:8, 9 *But God commendeth his love toward us, in that, while we were yet sinners, Christ died for us. Much more then, being now justified by his blood, we shall be saved from wrath through him.*

Colossians 2:13-14 *And you, being dead in your sins and the uncircumcision of your flesh, hath he quickened together with him, having forgiven you all trespasses; {14} Blotting out the handwriting of ordinances that was against us, which was contrary to us, and took it out of the way, nailing it to his cross;*

End

My Saviour

§

In deepest night I dreamed a tale of awful scope and dread,
More dark than any dream, yet dreamed upon my bed.

I saw myself did crush the thorns upon my Saviour's head;
Each soldier's face removed, my visage in their stead.

Through the streets and up the hill, my loving Saviour bleeding.
The hideous procession, was me and Satan leading.

Devils all around us, the priests and I could see,
Laughing jeering, dancing as He approached the tree.

And when I held the nail against my Saviour's palm,
My dream became the universe and everything was calm.

Triumphantly I raised the cross and secured it in the ground;
I turned to glory with the crowd, but no one was around.

So all alone I stare at Him, the one whose death is mine.
My guilt is flowing from his side through eternal sands of time.

Blood soaks my guilty hands, and stains my wretched face.
I kneel before the cross; my Saviour in my place.

He looks down, and commands my gaze into eyes of
all things true.
Forgive them, cries my Saviour, for they know not what they do.

end

Web of Addiction

§

INTRODUCTION TO THE *WEB OF Addiction*: This allegory is actually a letter written to an individual. A friend was destroying himself with alcohol. When spoken words fell only on deaf ears, I decided to write him a story. Eventually, my friend checked into an addiction treatment center where the letter circulated and impacted many persons.

Working as a chaplain in prison and rehabs, I read the letter to large groups, as well as discussing its relevance in private counselling sessions. The story lends itself very effectively to classroom settings, and always generates good discussion. Although the protagonist is an alcoholic, the story suits any form of life destroying addiction.

WHEN TEACHING OR USING THE STORY IN A GROUP SETTING:

Alert the audience to the allegorical nature of the tale before reading it out loud. In other words, define allegory and metaphor. Make sure your audience knows what you are talking about. This produces greater results.

The developing spider's web around Randy's backyard deck relates directly to Randy's life. The spiders' web is Randy's growing addiction problem. The actual time Randy is on the backyard deck is years, perhaps decades. He gradually loses control and becomes increasingly isolated from friends and family. Randy becomes oblivious to reality. Although some problems are recognized, he misinterprets and blames others. The weather is actually life's everyday problems. Things deteriorate, his lawn, his relationships with friends, even his marriage. The mosquito, in the end, is Randy who becomes hopelessly trapped in his addiction. Randy is left in the web, because only Randy knows if he wants to end his nightmare. Leaving the addict's web is a choice.

Web of Addiction

§

Ecclesiastes 9:12 For man also knoweth not his time: as the fishes that are taken in an evil net, and as the birds that are caught in the snare; so are the sons of men snared in an evil time, when it falleth suddenly upon them.

THE SPIDER ANCHORED HER WEB to the roof's edge then dropped several inches to the side of the house. Fastening her second foundation to the vinyl siding, she climbed back to the roof trailing a silver string. She repeated this procedure again and again until a pie shaped net hung alluringly on the corner of Randy's house.

Randy opened his patio door and stepped onto the deck and popped open a beer. After a long swallow, he sat down in a steel lawn chair and stretched his legs toward the edge of the deck. Randy noticed the spider. Setting the beer down on the table next to him, he went back inside the house and returned with a can of bug spray. Just as Randy aimed for the kill, a mosquito flew into the web. The spider attacked. Within seconds the spider cocooned the mosquito inside a compact little web. The cocoon prison shivered and quivered as the creature inside struggled for survival. Rethinking the spider's fate, Randy lowered his weapon.

"I hate mosquitoes," he said.

Randy finished his beer and walked down the steps into his back yard. Stooping over, he inserted his index finger into the lawn. The grass length reached his knuckle. Springtime always brought enough rain to ensure he mow twice a week. Forty minutes later the grass was cut, and he headed toward the deck. He stopped and plucked an off color green blade of grass, then soothingly brushed the surrounding area with the palm of his hand.

"Honey, dinner is ready," his wife, Betty, hollered through the screen.

"I think the mosquitoes are going to be bad this year," said Randy stepping inside the house. "They're already out in full force."

"It's all the rain," said Betty.

"I guess," he said scratching a tiny red bump on his arm.

The next day Randy examined the web. Three tiny cocoon prisons hung securely in the silky weave. He blew a stream of cigarette smoke at the web sending the spider scurrying to the roof.

"Good job," he said.

Sitting down, Randy thought the spider's web looked bigger. Not hugely so, but it did seem larger. He extinguished his cigarette in the ashtray and took a drink of beer. Tomorrow was the weekend, and for once in his life, he had nothing to do. Not even the grass needed cutting.

By Saturday afternoon, another web hung between the roof and house at the opposite end of the deck. Several mosquitoes had already met their hideous fate by the time Randy noticed this new addition to his backyard refuge.

"Well look at that," he said and walked over to the new web. He swirled the ice cubes in his glass with his finger and then flicked some liquid at the web. Droplets of whiskey hung trapped like the bugs and sparkled in the sun.

"There you go my little friend. Nothing like a cold drink after a big meal."

Several weeks later, two more webs appeared. Now there was one pie shaped web at each corner. Randy built his deck with large wooden posts positioned at both corners opposite the house. In-between the posts, stairs descended to the lawn. Another long, narrow spider web spanned high over the steps like a suspension bridge. It floated in the breeze, but stayed fastened to the posts.

Betty slid open the patio door and stepped onto the deck. She raised a broom reaching for the corner nearest the door. Randy grabbed the broom handle so abruptly he spilled his beer onto the deck's floor.

"What are you doing?" he said loudly.

"I'm getting rid of these spider webs," said Betty. "It's starting to look like a Halloween stage back here."

"No, you don't," said Randy, taking possession of the broom. "I haven't been bit by a mosquito in weeks. Those spiders do a great job."

"You either get rid of those spiders or you can keep this deck all to yourself."

"Don't be ridiculous," said Randy. But his wife retreated inside.

Randy opened the door and put the broom inside the house. Then he sat down and lit a cigarette. A mosquito, full of blood, left his neck and flew directly into a spider's web.

Eventually, spider webs sealed off the whole left side of the deck. The spiders constructed a series of diagonal strands from the roof's corner to the deck floor. Then they connected them with horizontal weaves. Their finished product produced a solid web wall the entire width of the deck nearly seven feet high, and dense enough to stop the cool winds of autumn. This allowed Randy to enjoy his backyard without the risk of taking a chill. He could even light a cigarette with the first match.

One day some old friends came to visit. Upon entering the back-yard, they viewed a vague silhouette of their friend behind the web. "Hey, Randy," one of them yelled, "Come out here in the open. We want to talk with you."

Randy peered through a peephole in web. He didn't feel like talking, and he believed the opaqueness of the web rendered him invisible. Refusing to move, he didn't answer and sipped his drink very quietly. Eventually, all his friends went away. Randy took a last drag on a cigarette and flicked the still burning butt onto the lawn.

In the end, solid web walls surrounded the entire deck; the spiders even built a roof. And with the roof in place, the deck provided year-long protection. Even under the hottest sun, the pouring rain, or severest winter blizzard, Randy felt no discomfort.

The big storm hit one summer evening as Randy drank alone on the deck. He thought he heard his wife calling him. He started to get up, felt dizzy and sat back down. "Betty should go to the doctor," he muttered. "Her voice gets weaker and weaker. I haven't heard her speak clearly for a long time."

When the dizziness subsided, Randy stood and gazed through a hole in the web. The tall, uncut grass bent as a gust of cold wind rushed in from the North. Randy drained his beer and pushed the bottle through the hole onto the lawn. He turned and walked toward the door of his house, but the door was gone. A web sealed off the entrance home.

Randy stood still. He knew the door was behind the web, but where? He turned around in a circle. "Maybe I'm at the wrong side?" he thought, so he walked slowly around the entire deck. All the webs looked the same. Even the hole he just pushed the bottle through was sealed over. Putting his hands against the web, he pushed with all his might. The web moved a little, but he couldn't break through. Randy identified a place where he thought the stairs to the back lawn were located, and walked to the opposite end of the deck. Crouching as if he were a sprinter, he took a deep breath and then ran fast as he could at the web. But he could not break through; the web held. And to make matters worse, the impact fused him to the spider's web. The soft silky fibers transformed into sticky strands of glue.

Several tiny spiders scurried across the deck floor and began to spin webbing around Randy's body. He yelled for his wife; she didn't answer. He yelled for his friends, but they had all gone away. The tiny spiders finished imprisoning their prey and disappeared.

Randy was sealed in the web as if inside a cocoon. He could still see, although dimly, through the silver strands of webbing covering his eyes. Suddenly the entire web, walls and ceiling, began to move in an out as if something huge was walking on it. Then a large, dark shadow appeared on the ceiling. Eight legs the size of small trees, connected to this shadow. Randy screams muffled against the web; the cocoon prison shivered and quivered as the creature inside struggled for survival.

End

Proverbs 14:8 *The wisdom of the prudent is to understand his way: but the folly of fools is deceit.*

1 Corinthians 3:18 *Let no man deceive himself. If any man among you seemeth to be wise in this world, let him become a fool, that he may be wise.*

Part Two
Divorce and Remarriage

§

FEW THINGS IN LIFE ARE as anguishing as a ruined marriage, unless it's the comments and instructions given to the divorced by religious people claiming to speak on God's behalf. Written for Christians who need to know what the Bible says about divorce, a no nonsense education using scriptures to answer your questions.

Divorce

§

MANY A SAINT FINDS HER/HIMSELF going through a heart wrenching divorce. Then again, when she/he starts over with a new spouse, heart-wrenching questions concerning what God thinks about the remarriage are always asked.

1. Does the Bible allow divorce?
2. Can Christians remarry and still be right with God?
3. Are divorced men forbidden to hold the office of pastor or deacon?

I reluctantly point out we are dealing with religious law. Although we live in an age of grace, in contrast to law, God still delivers rules pertaining to this present age. Telling Christians what God thinks about their divorce and remarriage is serious business. The pastor's and teacher's words affect people for whom Christ died and rose. Divorce and remarriage is an adult problem, and the Bible gives adult answers. Let us not error, as did many Pharisees in their handling of the scriptures. Let us not commit ourselves to such rigid legalism we neglect the weightier matters of God's law and purpose.

> **Matthew 23:23** *Woe unto you, scribes and Pharisees, hypocrites! for ye pay tithe of mint and anise and cummin, and have omitted*

the weightier matters of the law, judgment, mercy, and faith: these ought ye to have done, and not to leave the other undone.

If the law's weightier matters are judgment, mercy, and faith; surely the Church Age must include the same? Righteous judgment never kills mercy. When we must judge, let us judge wisely and with righteousness.

John 7:24 *Judge not according to the appearance, but judge righteous judgment.*

1 Corinthians 2:15 *But he that is spiritual judgeth all things, yet he himself is judged of no man.*

Remarriage after Spouse Dies

THE BIBLE IS VERY CLEAR, no binding laws against remarriage after a spouse dies. The only restriction is the surviving spouse marries a Christian.

> **Romans 7:1-3** *Know ye not, brethren, (for I speak to them that know the law,) how that the law hath dominion over a man as long as he liveth?* **2** *For the woman which hath an husband is bound by the law to her husband so long as he liveth; but if the husband be dead, she is loosed from the law of her husband.* **3** *So then if, while her husband liveth, she be married to another man, she shall be called an adulteress: but if her husband be dead, she is free from that law; so that she is no adulteress, though she be married to another man.*

> **1 Corinthians 7:39** *The wife is bound by the law as long as her husband liveth; but if her husband be dead, she is at liberty to be married to whom she will; only in the Lord.*

WHAT DOES THE BIBLE SAY ABOUT DIVORCE?

The Bible says a great deal about divorce. Trouble is not everyone understands it the same way. And even sadder, some people who understand choose to ignore the truth and teach their church policy instead.

Deuteronomy 24:1-4 When a man hath taken a wife, and married her, and it come to pass that she find no favour in his eyes, because he hath found some uncleanness in her: then let him write her a bill of divorcement, and give it in her hand, and send her out of his house. 2 And when she is departed out of his house, she may go and be another man's wife. 3 And if the latter husband hate her, and write her a bill of divorcement, and giveth it in her hand, and sendeth her out of his house; or if the latter husband die, which took her to be his wife; 4 Her former husband, which sent her away, may not take her again to be his wife, after that she is defiled; for that is abomination before the LORD: and thou shalt not cause the land to sin, which the LORD thy God giveth thee for an inheritance.

We see God did not forbid divorce. The law lays down a procedure to follow. Understand God allowing divorce does not mean God approves of divorce. Before continuing, methinks I hear someone yelling, *Old Testament verses should not be used in this study! That was the law, and Christians are not under the law.*

Romans 6:14 For sin shall not have dominion over you: for ye are not under the law, but under grace.

This kind of thinking is reasonable only until we learn what Jesus said about the Law. If one insists not to be under any law or religious rule based on *Romans 6:14*, how then could we adhere to any regulations on marriage or anything else? Furthermore, *Romans 7:1-3* was retrieved from the law, and God directs the whole discussion to those who know the law.

Matthew 5:17-19 Think not that I am come to destroy the law, or the prophets: I am not come to destroy, but to fulfil. 18 For verily I say unto you, Till heaven and earth pass, one jot or one tittle shall in no wise pass from the law, till all be fulfilled. 19 Whosoever therefore shall break one of these least commandments, and shall teach men so, he shall be called the least in the kingdom of heaven: but whosoever shall do and teach them, the same shall be called great in the kingdom of heaven.

Jesus did not disregard the Law. Everything He said about marriage and divorce was based on the law. Everything Jesus had Apostle Paul say about marriage and divorce was based on the law. In the Gospels, certain Pharisees brought the law to Jesus' attention.

Matthew 19:3-9 The Pharisees also came unto him, tempting him, and saying unto him, Is it lawful for a man to put away his wife for every cause? 4 And he answered and said unto them, Have ye not read, that he which made them at the beginning made them male and female, 5 And said, For this cause shall a man leave father and mother, and shall cleave to his wife: and they twain shall be one flesh? 6 Wherefore they are no more twain, but one flesh. What therefore God hath joined together, let not man put asunder. 7 They say unto him, Why did Moses then command to give a writing of divorcement, and to put her away? 8 He saith unto them, Moses because of the hardness of your hearts suffered you to put away your wives: but from the beginning it was not so. 9 And I say unto you, Whosoever shall put away his wife, except it be for fornication, and shall marry another, committeth adultery: and whoso marrieth her which is put away doth commit adultery.

To the question is it lawful for a man to put away his wife? We learned the holy word of God says *yes*. But the Pharisees asked if divorce was legal over *every cause*. And to that the answer is no. When Jesus says *from the beginning* he was directing their attention back to the creation of marriage. *Genesis. 2:21-24* He explains God's original and perfect intention wanted a marriage to be permanent.

The Pharisees ask *why did Moses then command to give a writing of divorcement, and to put her away?*

Between the *beginning* and Moses an event takes place we call the Fall. The Fall affected many things, including mankind's heart. And because of sinful and hardened hearts, God gave the laws of divorce. Although God's perfect will is marriage remains permanent, God acknowledges the fact bad marriages happen; therefore, God gives us laws and advice to regulate divorce.

Jesus states plainly in verse *Mt. 19:9*, one can lawfully divorce over fornication. We also learn consequences for putting away a spouse. If a person puts away his spouse and remarries, he commits adultery. Unless he/she divorce because a spouse is guilty of fornication! Fornication is legitimate Bible grounds for divorce. And the innocent person is not held accountable for committing adultery when he/she remarries. (See also Adultery and Responsibility in this study)

Some people interpret *Mat. 19:9* as allowing divorce, but not remarriage. Observe Jesus says and *shall marry another* in the same verse. The whole statement concerns someone who remarries. And the person who remarries commits adultery, unless his spouse committed fornication. Jesus gives a legal exception to the rule.

If a particular church forbids divorce when fornication has been committed, that church is wrong; the church directly opposes the clear teaching of Jesus Christ. I stress, however, because one retains the legal right to divorce, this does not necessarily mean one should divorce. A betrayed spouse also has the right to forgive and exercise the same charity God bestows to Israel and Christians over and over again. But that, of course, is a prayerful decision for the troubled couple to make, not a decision for the elders of the church.

EXCEPTIONS TO THE RULE
CONSIDER THESE COMMANDMENTS:

***Exodus 20:13 Thou** shalt not kill.*

***Exodus 21:12** He that smiteth a man, so that he die, shall be surely put to death.*

This is not a contradiction. Exceptional conditions, which exempt or seem to go against the general commandment involves righteous judgment. Although God commands men not to kill, a murderer is to be killed. Another example where killing would not be a transgression of the law is during war.

Divorce by Desertion

§

QUITE ANOTHER MATTER IS WHEN one person leaves for no apparent reason. Apostle Paul discusses this situation.

> *1 Corinthians 7:10-11 And unto the married I command, yet not I, but the Lord, Let not the wife depart from her husband: 11 But and if she depart, let her remain unmarried, or be reconciled to her husband: and let not the husband put away his wife*

Once a man and woman marry, they should stay married. However, if they do split up- hopefully the separation ends in a reunion of the couple. Notice the person who leaves is commanded to remain unmarried. Interestingly, that same command is not given to the one who does not want the divorce. Do not dismiss this as an insignificant omission. What does this one sided command mean? Are we to assume the one who does not want the divorce is commanded never to marry again? Even if his/her spouse never comes back! Before answering, consider what Paul says to unequally yoked couples (a believer married to an unbeliever).

> *1 Corinthians 7:12-15 But to the rest speak I, not the Lord: If any brother hath a wife that believeth not, and she be pleased to dwell with him, let him not put her away. 13 And the woman which hath an husband that believeth not, and if he be pleased to dwell with her,*

let her not leave him. **14** *For the unbelieving husband is sanctified by the wife, and the unbelieving wife is sanctified by the husband: else were your children unclean; but now are they holy.* **15 But if the unbelieving depart, let him depart. A brother or a sister is not under bondage in such cases: but God hath called us to peace.**

Focus on verse 7:15. If the unbeliever wants a divorce, give it to him. And the believer is not under bondage. What does not being under bondage mean? Bondage constrains or limits people; therefore. It must mean something that gives freedom and peace. Not being under bondage can only mean- not being subjected to the law directed at the one who departs. If the believer was commanded to remain alone for the rest of his/her life that would indeed be bondage. It would be like putting an innocent person in jail. God does not sentence innocent people to a life of loneliness and unfulfilled normal human passions; religious people do that, but not God.

Therefore, I conclude the believer may remarry (in the Lord) and have peace with God. This would be true also in the case where both husband and wife are believers. The one who does not want the divorce may remarry and be right with the Lord.

Adultery & Responsibility

A CAUSAL READING OF *MATTHEW 5:31, 32 and Matthew 19:9* may lead one to the conclusion Jesus is making exactly the same comments. But this is not true. Very important distinctions exist between the passages. For the reader's scrutiny, I print both verses below.

> ***Matthew 19:9*** *And I say unto you, Whosoever shall put away his wife, except it be for fornication, and shall marry another, committeth adultery: and whoso marrieth her which is put away doth commit adultery.*

> ***Matthew 5:32*** *But I say unto you, That whosoever shall put away his wife, saving for the cause of fornication, causeth her to commit adultery: and whosoever shall marry her that is divorced committeth adultery.*

In *Matthew 19:9* the emphasis is on the man who wants the divorce. And on the person who marries the divorced wife. Careful reading reveals Jesus does did not say that the wife commits adultery.

In *Matthew 5:31, 32-* the emphasis is on the divorced wife. This is very important. If a man divorces his wife when she is not guilty of fornication, he causes her to commit adultery; therefore, he is responsible for her adultery.

God expects the woman to get married again, that's why he says, *causeth her to commit adultery* - And, yes, technically the innocent wife partakes in adultery when she remarries. It's as if the sexual consummation of the new marriage terminates the old marriage. **But she is not guilty of adultery**. The unjust husband is held responsible for the sin. Notice the scripture says he caused the sin, not her. It is justifiable adultery.

To make this clearer, I appeal with an analogy: If an armed man breaks into your home and threatens your family's life and you shoot him and kill him. You have technically committed murder. But under the law, you are not guilty of murder, because he caused you to do it. He was responsible for your actions. It's called justifiable homicide.

Defining Adultery

EVERYONE KNOWS WHAT ADULTERY IS, or do they? The Bible identifies four types of adultery:

1. Spiritual Adultery
2. Classic Adultery
3. Adultery committed in the Heart
4. Justifiable Adultery

#1 SPIRITUAL ADULTERY

Jeremiah 3:8-9 And I saw, when for all the causes whereby backsliding Israel committed adultery I had put her away, and given her a bill of divorce; yet her treacherous sister Judah feared not, but went and played the harlot also. 9 And it came to pass through the lightness of her whoredom, that she defiled the land, and committed adultery with stones and with stocks.

God uses the terms adultery, fornication, and whoredom numerous times throughout the Bible to describe Israel's idolatry and backsliding. Adultery typifies the highest act of treason a person can commit against her/his spouse. Nothing crushes an innocent and loving wife/husband as does this sin. Nor is there anything that so jeopardizes a relationship; thus, God chose this sin to metaphorically describe his own feelings when believers step out on him. By this I mean when believers love or worship people or things more than God. Not to be overlooked is the fact that God is divorced.

#2 CLASSIC ADULTERY

> **Leviticus 20:10** *And the man that committeth adultery with another man's wife, even he that committeth adultery with his neighbour's wife, the adulterer and the adulteress shall surely be put to death*

Classic adultery is what most people think about when they hear the word adultery. A married person steps out on his/her spouse and has sexual relations with another person. As you can see from the verse, the consequences could be quite serious; however, let the bible student ponder this curious fact. There is no biblical record of the death penalty being carried out for adultery, but numerous accounts of the guilty being shown mercy exist. Consider: Judah, Reuben, David, and Samson, Gomer, the adulteress in *John 8*, and countless un-named Israelites. God manifests grace under the law numerous times. This provides a good reference when people mistakenly believe the God of the Old Testament is different than the God of the New Testament; Jesus is very consistent. Mercy is one of God's attributes.

> **Hebrews 13:8** *Jesus Christ the same yesterday, and to day, and for ever.*

#3 ADULTERY COMMITTED IN THE HEART.

> **Matthew 5:28** *But I say unto you, That whosoever looketh on a woman to lust after her hath committed adultery with her already in his heart.*

Jesus says when a person imagines he/she is having sex with someone other than his/her spouse commits adultery. How many Christians commit this adultery? Would the gentlemen answer first please?

#4 JUSTIFIABLE ADULTERY

Matthew 5:32 But I say unto you, That whosoever shall put away his wife, saving for the cause of fornication, causeth her to commit adultery: and whosoever shall marry her that is divorced committeth adultery.

When a person divorces his/her innocent spouse and the spouse remarries, the innocent spouse is not held accountable.

Christians should ponder these four kinds of adultery. They are all biblical, so let's not ignore them. As Christians judge others, isn't it amazing how they focus on the adultery they have not done? And then interpret all the relating scriptures from the premise of their supposed innocence? Perhaps it's time to back up, or face up to our own self-righteousness. Maybe there is more Pharisee in us than we realize? Really now, haven't you ever noticed the sins you don't do are the worst ones?

Romans 2:21-23 Thou therefore which teachest another, teachest thou not thyself? thou that preachest a man should not steal, dost thou steal? 22 Thou that sayest a man should not commit adultery, dost thou commit adultery? thou that abhorrest idols, dost thou commit sacrilege? 23 Thou that makest thy boast of the law, through breaking the law dishonourest thou God?

Impossible Marriage

WHAT ABOUT SITUATIONS OTHER THAN FORNICATION WHICH MAKES STAYING IN A MARRIAGE IMPOSSIBLE? THINKING CHRISTIANS, SHOULD REALIZE SITUATIONS exist besides infidelity that are intolerable. All too often Christian leadership seems afraid to exercise a little clear thinking outside their denomination's official policy. Unless an answer to some difficult life problem is very simply spelled out, they are reluctant to even offer one. Or worse, clinging to partial understanding or church policy, they give hurtful advice. The intellectual equivalent is like people who don't believe Jesus is God, because there isn't a verse that says exactly *Jesus Christ is God* (spelled out in one and two syllable words). Or they won't believe God is a trinity, because there isn't a verse that says *God is a trinity*. Absolutely, the Bible teaches both the deity of Jesus Christ and the triune nature of God, but it takes some reasoning and thinking skills on the reader's behalf to comprehend those truths. Just because the Bible does not present every possible destructive scenario for marriage, this does not mean we ignore the problems when we see them.

Take, for example, the true story of a Christian woman whose husband physically abused her and their children. This situation went on for years and years and was getting worse. She actually feared for her life. The woman asked her Pastor if God would permit a divorce in such a circumstance. Although, the Pastor felt very sorry for the woman, his advice was to stay married. Why? Because he truly believed the Bible only allows divorce when adultery is committed. As far as he knew, child and spouse abuse were not biblically lawful reasons. And, according to this pastor, if she left him, she should stay alone for the rest of her life (in poverty).

Many different behaviors deny the marriage and mock God. For Christian leadership to sanction intolerable situations and think they are obeying God is absolutely pathetic. When mistreatment and abuse in a marriage reaches an intolerable level, something must be done. We must use our brains and judge wisely and with righteousness. Serious abuse violates:

> *1 Timothy 5:8 But if any provide not for his own, and specially for those of his own house, he hath denied the faith, and is worse than an infidel.*

> *1 Peter 3:7 Likewise, ye husbands, dwell with them according to knowledge, giving honour unto the wife, as unto the weaker vessel, and as being heirs together of the grace of life; that your prayers be not hindered.*

> *1 Corinthians 7:2-4 Nevertheless, to avoid fornication, let every man have his own wife, and let every woman have her own husband. 3 Let the husband render unto the wife due benevolence: and likewise also the wife unto the husband. 4 The wife hath not power of her own body, but the husband: and likewise also the husband hath not power of his own body, but the wife.*

> *Ephesians 5:21-29 Submitting yourselves one to another in the fear of God. 22 Wives, submit yourselves unto your own husbands, as unto the Lord. 23 For the husband is the head of the wife, even as Christ is the head of the church: and he is the saviour of the body. 24 Therefore as the church is subject unto Christ, so let the wives be to*

their own husbands in every thing. 25 Husbands, love your wives, even as Christ also loved the church, and gave himself for it; 26 That he might sanctify and cleanse it with the washing of water by the word, 27 That he might present it to himself a glorious church, not having spot, or wrinkle, or any such thing; but that it should be holy and without blemish. 28 So ought men to love their wives as their own bodies. He that loveth his wife loveth himself. 29 For no man ever yet hated his own flesh; but nourisheth and cherisheth it, even as the Lord the church:

Just as modern day secular lawyers wrestle with American law, religious leaders must, at times, wrestle with God's laws. Too many times our secular judges, for the sake of obeying one or two lines in the American Constitution, compromise the entire intent of the Constitution. In America today, we have so failed with handling constitutional law; our courts have been reduced to being only a legal system. But the intent was for our courts to be a justice system. Justice has been sacrificed for law.

In the Bible, the Pharisees were guilty of this same thing. They were so careful to obey the letter of the law they lost sight of the spirit of the law. Jesus said they strained at gnats and swallowed camels. They reduced Judaism to a religious system nearly void of righteousness and wise judgment.

Christianity, especially concerning divorce, has become similarly unwise. Problems such as: child abuse, physical/emotional spousal abuse, selfishness to the point of not even providing adequate food and clothing, sexual abuse this includes everything from bizarre perversions to denying sex to one's spouse, etc. – none of these behaviors may have a scripture depicting the exact description of the sin, but all can become so destructive (even life threatening) something has to be done.

One of the biggest problems the Pharisees had with Jesus Christ is they truly believed Jesus and his disciples broke the law in regards to the Sabbath day. God had given a clear, concise law, and the church leadership understood every word in the verse. Since Jesus worked on the Sabbath, Jesus broke the law. To the Pharisees, the reason did not matter. God gave them a law, and they were absolutely incapable of assessing the situation with moral clarity or righteous judgment. This is exactly the same problem religious people have with divorce. Consider the passage below.

> *Matthew 12:1-5 At that time Jesus went on the sabbath day through the corn; and his disciples were an hungred, and began to pluck the ears of corn, and to eat. 2 But when the Pharisees saw it, they said unto him, Behold, thy disciples do that which is not lawful to do upon the sabbath day. 3 But he said unto them, Have ye not read what David did, when he was an hungred, and they that were with him; 4 How he entered into the house of God, and did eat the shewbread, which was not lawful for him to eat, neither for them which were with him, but only for the priests? 5 Or have ye not read in the law, how that on the sabbath days the priests in the temple profane the sabbath, and are blameless?*

Notice Jesus does not deny working on the Sabbath day. He justifies his actions with righteous reasoning. Jesus cites historical examples from the Old Testament where circumstances forced believers to break the law, but God did not hold them accountable. Due to extraordinary circumstances, they were blameless! In other words they were not guilty!

> *Matthew 12:9-14 And when he was departed thence, he went into their synagogue: 10 And, behold, there was a man which had his hand withered. And they asked him, saying, Is it lawful to heal on the sabbath days? that they might accuse him. 11 And he said unto them, What man shall there be among you, that shall have one sheep, and if it fall into a pit on the sabbath day, will he not*

lay hold on it, and lift it out? **12** *How much then is a man bet-*
ter than a sheep? Wherefore it is lawful to do well on the sabbath
days. **13** *Then saith he to the man, Stretch forth thine hand. And*
he stretched it forth; and it was restored whole, like as the other. **14**
Then the Pharisees went out, and held a council against him, how
they might destroy him.

Again we see under special circumstances, the law of not working on
the Sabbath day is set aside. Look at verse 12, Jesus actually declares
the act of doing good work on the Sabbath day lawful. When con-
fronted with situations demanding righteous judgment, the religious
leadership was dumbfounded.

Today many church leaders have become Pharisees, their religious reasoning is void of mercy and understanding. Their commit-
ment to obeying religious law, which is often private interpretation
and tradition, violates righteousness. They shoot the wounded when
they should be applying the balm of Gilead. Like Job's three friends,
they are physicians of no value.

Matthew 23:23-24 Woe unto you, scribes and Pharisees, hypo-
crites! for ye pay tithe of mint and anise and cummin, and have
omitted the weightier matters of the law, judgment, mercy, and
faith: these ought ye to have done, and not to leave the other undone.
24 Ye blind guides, which strain at a gnat, and swallow a camel

The Guilty

§

WHAT ABOUT THE GUILTY ADULTERER? What about Christians who absolutely caused the divorce? What about those not married who commit fornication?

Unfortunately, many Christians put themselves in guilty situations. Their selfishness and immoral behavior has no defense. Make no mistake; the sin is a bad one. Adultery and Fornication (sex outside of marriage) is addressed in this section.

> *1 Corinthians 6:18-20 Flee fornication. Every sin that a man doeth is without the body; but he that committeth fornication sinneth against his own body. 19 What? know ye not that your body is the temple of the Holy Ghost which is in you, which ye have of God, and ye are not your own? 20 For ye are bought with a price: therefore glorify God in your body, and in your spirit, which are God's.*

The first thing a guilty person needs to do is repent. Repentance, however, may not fix the damage. Consequences must be faced. Sin can be devastating. Never forget, however, Jesus Christ puts repentant Christians' lives back together. Let's examine the life of one guilty person in the Bible. I have selected the familiar story of the Samaritan woman at the well.

> *John 4:16-19 Jesus saith unto her, Go, call thy husband, and come hither. 17 The woman answered and said, I have no husband. Jesus*

*said unto her, Thou hast well said, I have no husband: **18** For thou hast had five husbands; and he whom thou now hast is not thy husband: in that saidst thou truly. **19** The woman saith unto him, Sir, I perceive that thou art a prophet.*

This is a remarkable discourse. **Jesus acknowledges the woman has had five husbands.** And he acknowledges her present relationship with a man to whom she is not married. I now step off into dangerous territory. I must do some inferring (interpreting) about the text. But I proceed prayerfully and reasonably:

Five marriages! I think it unreasonable to assume her five past husbands all died, and she remarried with the blessing of God's law; therefore, I assume she has been divorced. I also assume this woman is no stranger to the sin of adultery. Concerning her present relationship with a man, I assume she is not cohabiting as a celibate. In other words, she is fornicating with her boyfriend.

When Jesus says *thou hast had five husbands* he acknowledged five separate marriages. This is a very important statement. The Lord accepted the marriages as legally binding. The real evidence is learned from observing what Jesus says about her boyfriend. By stating the man she lived with was not her husband, Jesus tells us plainly he still judged between being married and just living together.

God's acknowledging numerous marriages does not mean he condones the events preceding the union. God accepted King David's marriage to Bathsheba, but he certainly did not approve of the sins that brought them together. And even though God *put away David's sin, 2 Sa. 12:13,* David carried the consequences for the rest of his life. Nothing could bring back the lives of the men David murdered in his attempt to cover the sin. David also severely damaged his testimony. David's reputation being badly damaged (even till this day) manifests some disturbing facts about believers' willingness, perhaps even our capability to forgive others. In my opinion, many Christian leaders are more worried about their own religion and church policy- far more than they are righteous judgment. The Bible is only minimally studied or considered. Religious traditions become more important than scripture.

Many Christians have a difficult time believing God honors a new marriage of guilty persons. But it's just one more human condition that needs forgiveness. A thief can repent and stop stealing. A liar can stop lying. And an adulterer can repent, find forgiveness, and remarry. It's only some religious men and women that do not accept the new marriage, not God.

Some Christians point to *Romans 7:3* as evidence for not accepting remarriage. The verse does make a strong statement against a guilty person. God is clearly calling the individual an adulterer. Still, it is the wrong conclusion to believe God does not accept the marriage.

> **Romans 7:1-3** *Know ye not, brethren,* **(for I speak to them that know the law,)** *how that the law hath dominion over a man as long as he liveth? 2 For the woman which hath an husband is bound by the law to her husband so long as he liveth; but if the husband be dead, she is loosed from the law of her husband. 3 So then if, while her husband liveth, she be married to another man, she shall be called an adulteress: but if her husband be dead, she is free from that law; so that she is no adulteress, though she be married to another man.*

The first two verses deal with a woman's right to marry after her husband dies. But notice the parenthetical reference to the law in verse one. Those who know the law acknowledge legal reasons for divorce. Since the remark is made to those who know the law, let us look to the law. *Deuteronomy 24:1-4* gives legal permission for the divorced wife to remarry. Remember she was put away for some uncleanness. That uncleanness could well have been legal grounds for divorce, thus making the woman guilty. On the other hand, the divorce might be largely the husband's fault. Either way, God accepted the new marriage; God said she could go and be the wife of another man.

> **Deuteronomy 24:1-3** *When a man hath taken a wife, and married her, and it come to pass that she find no favour in his eyes, because he hath found some uncleanness in her: then let him write her a bill of divorcement, and give it in her hand, and send her out of his house.* **2 And when she is departed out of his house, she may go and be another man's wife. 3** *And if the latter husband hate her, and write her a bill of divorcement, and giveth it in her hand, and sendeth her out of his house; or if the latter husband die, which took her to be his wife;*

Considering *Romans 7:3* - How can a person be called an adulteress when she is married? By definition, adultery can only be done outside marriage. We have a paradox. The correct interpretation cannot erase established law. Nor can we forget Jesus acknowledging the Samaritan woman's five husbands. Therefore, I conclude when a guilty person is divorced and remarried: It seems the first act of sexual intercourse with his/ her new spouse is considered adultery. Sort of a physical announcement the first marriage is terminated. It is also the consummation of the new marriage. But from that point on, the sexual union is sanctified as in all legal marriages. God acknowledges the new marriage, and he expects the new couple to honor it as well.

As far as the statement, *she shall be called an adulteress.* Apparently it was her adultery that caused the divorce, so she certainly was an adulteress. But if she confesses her sin to God and repents she is forgiven. For Christians who are not convinced, and still believe God never accepts a new marriage. How do you explain Jesus acknowledging the five husbands of the woman at the well? Furthermore, think about the ramifications of an alternative interpretation. Do you believe divorced and remarried persons commit adultery every time they engage in sexual intercourse?

Do you believe every time David had relations with Bathsheba he was committing adultery? That would make King Solomon a bastard. Would God have a bastard build his temple? King Solomon cannot be considered illegitimate.

> **Deuteronomy 23:2** *A bastard shall not enter into the congregation of the LORD; even to his tenth generation shall he not enter into the congregation of the LORD.*

I have a very well educated Christian friend who emphatically disagrees with me about divorce and remarriage. Concerning David's marriage to Bathsheba, he believes the only reason God accepted it was because Bathsheba's husband was dead. The problem with his reasoning is David murdered her husband. To this, my friend replies, God forgave him of the murder so everything was legal. Ironically, his answer does contain some truth. His reasoning threads the needle concerning the law of divorce, but it ignores the law concerning murder, as well as the law regarding the consequence of adultery. Hence a perfect example of using law to judge un-righteously.

Here is an amazing thing to me, my friend acknowledges the legality of King David's marriage, but condemns marriages of divorced and remarried Christians. Would murdering a person's spouse legitimize adultery today? NO! And it didn't justify David either. It made things worse. There are lots of Christians like my friend. All they comprehend is a part of the law that seems to side with their ethics. In King David's case, since the law directly says after a man is dead, his wife may remarry and be guiltless- this they understand. Yet everyone ignores what another law says about murder. They are too prideful and judgmental to judge with wisdom and righteousness. And they seem to ignore God's mercy and forgiveness is what put everything back together, not laws.

Bathsheba's husband being dead did not make David's marriage accepted by God. God's mercy and forgiveness made the marriage legal! If people can accept God forgiving a murderer, why can't they accept God forgiving adultery or divorce? The evidence many Christians do not comprehend God's great attributes of mercy and forgiveness-- is their constant ignoring of *1ˢᵗ John 1:9*. (For anyone other than them) As King David found mercy and forgiveness, so can Christians today.

> *1 John 1:8-9 If we say that we have no sin, we deceive ourselves, and the truth is not in us. 9 If we confess our sins, he is faithful and just to forgive us our sins, and to cleanse us from all unrighteousness.*

1 John 1:8-9 is a tremendous truth and promise to Christians. This is not a salvation verse; it is a Christian getting right with God verse. Another passage dealing with the guilty is found in John's Gospel chapter eight.

> *John 8:1-12 Jesus went unto the mount of Olives. 2 And early in the morning he came again into the temple, and all the people came unto him; and he sat down, and taught them. 3 And the scribes and Pharisees brought unto him a woman taken in adultery; and when they had set her in the midst, 4 They say unto him, Master, this woman was taken in adultery, in the very act. 5 Now Moses in the law commanded us, that such should be stoned: but what sayest thou? 6 This they said, tempting him, that they might have to accuse him. But Jesus stooped down, and with his finger wrote on the ground, as though he heard them not. 7 So when they continued asking him, he lifted up himself, and said unto them, He that is without sin among you, let him first cast a stone at her. 8 And again he stooped down, and wrote on the ground. 9 And they which heard it, being convicted by their own conscience, went out one by one, beginning at the eldest, even unto the last: and Jesus was left alone, and the woman standing in the midst. 10 When Jesus had lifted up himself, and saw none but the woman, he said unto her,*

Woman, where are those thine accusers? hath no man condemned thee? 11 She said, No man, Lord. And Jesus said unto her, Neither do I condemn thee: go, and sin no more. 12 Then spake Jesus again unto them, saying, I am the light of the world: he that followeth me shall not walk in darkness, but shall have the light of life.

Sure the Pharisees set the whole thing up. The Pharisees probably targeted some lonely married woman (*Maybe an arranged marriage to a man three times her age?*). They employed some good-looking fellow to go after her with false promises. And then when the right moment arrived, they burst into the bedroom, and dragged her off to Jesus. Need I mention they conveniently forgot to bring the man? Whatever happened, Jesus knew all about it. Notice he never told anyone they couldn't stone her. According to the law, one could argue they had the legal right to throw the rocks. So what if the man wasn't there; they knew who he was. They could take care of him later. I wonder what would have happened if the potential stone throwers had been a group of modern Christian preachers.

The law says an adulterer and the adulteress should be put to death *Le. 20:10*. And Jesus stated he came not to destroy the law, but to fulfill. Why didn't Jesus name the man, and then order them both stoned? Dare we ask the ludicrous question, did the Lord break the law? For the Pharisee who can't see past the instruction of one verse, his answer would be yes. For the Christian who refuses to see judgment, mercy, and faith are the weightier matters of God's law, his answer would be yes. Of course, we know Jesus handled the matter in a way that glorified righteousness and fulfilled the law.

Are you guilty of adultery, a wicked imagination, fornication, or some other sin that destroyed your marriage or ruined the marriage of someone else? Perhaps your sin is secret, but breaks your fellowship with God? Read and listen to the words of the great I AM as he addresses a guilty sinner.

John 8:11 *She said, No man, Lord. And Jesus said unto her,* **Neither do I condemn thee: go, and sin no more**

You must confess your sin to God. Repent. Make things right as you can. Get on with your life. Serve God.

1 John 1:9 *If we confess our sins, he is faithful and just to forgive us our sins, and to cleanse us from all unrighteousness*

Proverbs 28:13 *He that covereth his sins shall not prosper: but whoso confesseth and forsaketh them shall have mercy*

Marriage

WHEN DOES GOD CONSIDER A MAN AND WOMAN MARRIED?

MOST PEOPLE ARE SURPRISED WHEN they learn a marriage ceremony is not in the Bible. Scripture acknowledges and discuss marriages, but decrees no procedure or specific ceremony. This leads to the logical question, when exactly does God consider a man and woman married? Some Christians believe the act of sexual intercourse, alone, determines marriage. Although I disagree with that position, it is not as silly as it may seem. Consider this warning by Paul, and then compare the passage to God's initial statement on marriage.

> *1 Corinthians 6:15-16 Know ye not that your bodies are the members of Christ? shall I then take the members of Christ, and make them the members of an harlot? God forbid. 16 What? know ye not that he which is joined to an harlot is one body? for two, saith he, shall be one flesh.*

> *Genesis 2:24 Therefore shall a man leave his father and his mother, and shall cleave unto his wife: and they shall be one flesh.*

The idea becoming one through sexual union is implicit in both texts, thus the conclusion; *becoming one equals marriage* is established. To refute the teaching, I again refer to the Samaritan woman at the well. Jesus acknowledged five different husbands, and He made the distinction between a live in boyfriend and a married man. Jesus also acknowledged weddings as proper social functions. Indeed, he performed his first miracle at a marriage in Cana of Galilee. With weddings acknowledged as social, legal, and civil events, they obviously represent something different than sexual intercourse. The physical union, however, did finalize or consummate a legal marriage. But all things done decently and in order. The warning in *1 Cor. 6:15, 16* is serious. There is no such thing as casual sex. If people are having sex outside of marriage, they are living in sin.

Hebrews 13:4 *Marriage is honourable in all, and the bed undefiled: but whoremongers and adulterers God will judge.*

Staying Single

Matthew 19:10-12 His disciples say unto him, If the case of the man be so with his wife, it is not good to marry. 11 But he said unto them, All men cannot receive this saying, save they to whom it is given. 12 For there are some eunuchs, which were so born from their mother's womb: and there are some eunuchs, which were made eunuchs of men: and there be eunuchs, which have made themselves eunuchs for the kingdom of heaven's sake. He that is able to receive it, let him receive it.

JUST SO WE ALL KNOW, a eunuch is a man without testicles. The testicles produce a hormone called testosterone. This hormone is largely responsible for sexual desire. Kings, in old times, made the men who watched their harems eunuchs. A birth defect can also cause this unfortunate physical condition. An accepted historical truth is eunuchs do not marry.

When Jesus says some men made themselves eunuchs for the kingdom of heaven's sake, he means some men deny themselves the pleasure of a wife so they may serve the Lord more devotedly. He did not mean some men should castrate themselves. Jesus did not order anyone vow never to marry. Only religious doctrines outside the Bible forbid marriage. Basically, Jesus says, if you can handle staying single, good for you, you'll be able to serve God with unique devotion. But it is certainly not for everyone. Some people choose a life of celibacy and then, years later, change their minds and decide to get married. Nothing is wrong with them changing their mind. Apostle Paul, who elected not to have a wife, teaches this as well.

__1 Corinthians__ 7:7-9 For I would that all men were even as I myself. But every man hath his proper gift of God, one after this manner, and another after that. 8 I say therefore to the unmarried and widows, It is good for them if they abide even as I. 9 But if they cannot contain, let them marry: for it is better to marry than to burn.

__1 Corinthians__ 7:25-28 Now concerning virgins I have no commandment of the Lord: yet I give my judgment, as one that hath obtained mercy of the Lord to be faithful. 26 I suppose therefore that this is good for the present distress, I say, that it is good for a man so to be. 27 Art thou bound unto a wife? seek not to be loosed. Art thou loosed from a wife? seek not a wife. 28 But and if thou marry, thou hast not sinned; and if a virgin marry, she hath not sinned. Nevertheless such shall have trouble in the flesh: but I spare you.

__1 Corinthians__ 7:32-33 But I would have you without carefulness. He that is unmarried careth for the things that belong to the Lord, how he may please the Lord: 33 But he that is married careth for the things that are of the world, how he may please his wife.

I see no need to give lengthy commentary on these verses. The gist of the teaching is to serve God. Some people can do a better job if they stay single; most of us cannot. Marriage has serious consequences. Marriage can be wonderful and very fulfilling in many ways, but married people also experience numerous problems they would not experience if they stayed single. (And all the married folks say- Amen) Being married is no guarantee of not being lonely. And being married is certainly no guarantee for being happy.

Forgiveness

§

FORGIVENESS REMAINS A STRUGGLE; ESPECIALLY for the betrayed; infidelity is a painful ordeal. Yet, forgiveness remains a main doctrine and component of Christianity; it becomes essential for spiritual and emotional growth. Forgiveness is also a fundamental component of grace. All Christians need to forgive others, it is not an option. In our transformation to be like Christ, we must learn to forgive. Below is checklist on forgiveness; I pray it helps.

1. Forgive does not mean forget. You do not forget what happened even when you forgive the person. No one expects you to forget.
2. You do not forgive people because they deserve it; you forgive people because you deserve it. Otherwise you keep reliving the hurt and pain.
3. Ask God to allow you to forgive this person/ group/etc. *Lord, help me to forgive- the guilty are in your hands. I need to move on with my life.*

Example: I was talking with a person who had something terrible, humiliating, and demoralizing done to him/her. Listening to this person's vivid and traumatizing telling of the ordeal made me think the crime happened only a few weeks previous (if not only a few days) however,- upon further counseling, I learned the actual event happened 22 years earlier.

Not forgiving the guilty person forces the victim to keep reliving the pain. In worst cases, not forgiving allows the guilty to keep doing the deed over and over to you. Why allow this kind of victory to an assailant? In all likelihood, the guilty person moves on with life and has forgotten all about you? I need to stress here- most acts of forgiveness are not for notorious or criminal sadists; rather, our forgiveness is for more average human sinful situations. The moral principle and healing benefits of forgiveness, however, remain the same.

A serious mistake- Some people don't want to forgive because they receive gratification by their constant retelling the incident. They deceive themselves into believing this is helping them heal. They want other people to anguish along with them and truly dislike the person who hurt them. A sort of revenge- pretending they get even by letting more and more people know. Although this is self-destructive, it is very common. It is called bitterness.

No matter what was done to you, no matter how anguishing the betrayal, how unjust or unfair. Put it alongside of how many times Jesus Christ has forgiven you- (even for sins since you were saved) Ask God to allow you to forgive this person/ group/etc. Lord, help me to forgive- the guilty are in your hands. I need to move on with my life.

Deacons & Pastors

§

ARE DIVORCED MEN FORBIDDEN TO hold the office of pastor (bishop) or deacon?

The question: Who is eligible for pastor or deacon comes up from time to time in almost all churches. Texts from *1st Timothy and Titus* give criteria from which churches draw their policies. Let the Christian notice God lists numerous concerns. Why the *one wife* takes precedent over all other issues is actually quite interesting. Generally, there are two interpretations regarding the one wife issue. Before looking closely at the whole biblical criteria, I provide summary of the two opposing religious positions.

POSITION #1

The majority of church leaders believe if a man has been divorced, he is not eligible for either pastor or deacon. It does not matter if the man has only one wife at the time he is considering the office. If he has ever been divorced, regardless of the reason, he is ineligible. A divorced-remarried man has had more than one wife and that would violate the scripture.

POSITION #2

The minority opinion believes a man must have one wife when he is called to office. A remarried man has only one wife. Even though he had another wife in the past, after the divorce, she is no longer his wife; therefore, the one wife criterion is fulfilled. The minority opinion points out a common Middle Eastern practice was polygamy. This is still true today. And this is what the one wife order forbid.

The minority opinion argues those holding position #1 are inconsistent in their one wife per lifetime interpretation, because they accept remarried widowers. The scripture emphasis is on one wife-**the criteria does not excuse widows to remarry**; that allowance is interpretation. If one allows a remarried widower, then the man has had more than one wife. Why church leaders acknowledge this exception allowed by the law, but then not accept another legal exception is an obvious contradiction. Jesus allowed legal remarriage in the case of fornication. The majority justifies the exception based on *Romans 7:1-3 and 1st Corinthians 7:39*. Peculiarly, no one holding position #1 seems to mind that both those scriptures retrieved from Old Testament law are considered valid- and Jesus' teaching, declaring fornication a legitimate biblical reason for divorce is ignored. Why Christian leaders try and obey an Old Testament law, while they deny a New Testament doctrine taught by Jesus Christ is quite fascinating.

Biblical Criteria for Being Pastors/Deacon

1 Timothy 3:1-12 This is a true saying, If a man desire the office of a bishop, he desireth a good work. 2 A bishop then must be blameless, the husband of one wife, vigilant, sober, of good behaviour, given to hospitality, apt to teach; 3 Not given to wine, no striker, not greedy of filthy lucre; but patient, not a brawler, not covetous; 4 One that ruleth well his own house, having his children in subjection with all gravity; 5 (For if a man know not how to rule his own house, how shall he take care of the church of God?) 6 Not a novice, lest being lifted up with pride he fall into the condemnation of the devil. 7 Moreover he must have a good report of them which are without; lest he fall into reproach and the snare of the devil. 8

Likewise must the deacons be grave, not doubletongued, not given to much wine, not greedy of filthy lucre; 9 Holding the mystery of the faith in a pure conscience. 10 And let these also first be proved; then let them use the office of a deacon, being found blameless. 11 Even so must their wives be grave, not slanderers, sober, faithful in all things. 12 Let the deacons be the husbands of one wife, ruling their children and their own houses well.

Titus 1:6-9 If any be blameless, the husband of one wife, having faithful children not accused of riot or unruly. 7 For a bishop must be blameless, as the steward of God; not selfwilled, not soon angry, not given to wine, no striker, not given to filthy lucre; 8 But a lover of hospitality, a lover of good men, sober, just, holy, temperate; 9 Holding fast the faithful word as he hath been taught, that he may be able by sound doctrine both to exhort and to convince the gainsayers.

Quite a list isn't it? Is there one pastor or deacon that could honestly say he steadfastly fulfills these requirements? Let's be kind and only trace his life back to the second year after he got saved. Who among us fulfills all those requirements?

Why do we allow men who were once drunks, but have since repented, to be pastors? Has there ever been a pastor who loved money? Do we accept a pastor who was once self-willed? How about a pastor whose children do not exemplify Christian character? Have you ever known a deacon who is not apt to teach? Many pastors actually feel at ease with deacons not capable of teaching. How serious and inquiring do we really get about our deacons? So a man has never been divorced; has he ever committed adultery? Has he ever committed fornication? Do we even ask them if they did? We won't even talk about being blameless, or covetous, patient, and holy.

The point is this: If we hold a man accountable for having a bad marriage in the past, why is he not accountable for all those other requirements for which he was once guilty? **Why does repentance**

fix everything on the list, but divorce? The hypocrisy on divorce by church leadership is overt and embarrassing. The truth is many churches do not consider the whole list. It seems church leaders single out the one requirement they have met and made it nonnegotiable. In other words, the one thing for which they are not guilty. Again I ask the readers- Have you ever noticed the sins you don't do are the worst ones?

CONSIDER THIS:

Two young people, Steven and Danielle, grow up in church and get saved in their early teenage years at church camp. A few years later, they fall in love and get married, (both were virgins), and both feel called into Christian service. Steven in particular is certain God called him be a pastor. They have children and everything is going along fine- but then WHAM, divorce happens. Five years go by and both people put their lives back together. They remarry (to different people) and are still active in church work.

Steven is a gifted speaker, educated at Bible College, and still believes he should be a preacher. When he discusses his calling with the pastor and church elders he is told "Sorry- but since you were divorced you cannot be a pastor, or a deacon, in fact we are going to pray seriously and discuss whether or not we should even allow you to teach Sunday School."

CONSIDER THIS:

Two young people, Joseph and Diane, (amazingly at the same church as Steven and Danielle) Although, Joseph gets saved, after a few years backslides and follows his flesh. Joseph gets involved with crime and drugs, and did many things that need not be mentioned here. Joseph mocked God and sexual promiscuity was a way of life. Joseph may even have a child, but that was a wild summer and all those wild parties, and no one can be sure. So why investigate? One can turn over too many rocks, if you know what I mean? Although Joseph had numerous partners and even a live in girl-friend, he never married.

Years go by and God's conviction compels Joseph to repent and get right with the Lord. He gets married and has children. He is a decent speaker and feels called to the ministry. He approaches the pastor and tells him about what God has called him to do. The pastor is excited for Joseph and encourages him to pursue God's calling in his life. In the meantime, Joseph is asked to teach Sunday school. And all the elders agree, *after checking 1Timothy 3 and Titus*, Joseph remains a good prospect to be a deacon in the future.

MODERN CHURCH JUDGMENT AND CONCLUSIONS:
In religious reality, the two most important qualifications for leadership positions.

1. He Must Tithe
2. He Was Never Divorced

Tithing is not mentioned in either *1ˢᵗ Timothy or Titus*. But it is covered, some would insist, under statements like being faithful, not greedy, or covetous. That is arguably true, but curiously, the specific doctrine most important to many church leaders is not mentioned specifically by God.

Dear Brothers in the Lord, if God calls you into service do not let religious men dissuade you. Serve God. How many God called pastors refuse to serve because they obey religious doctrines of men? Search the scriptures and prove what God says about requirements.

CHAPTER NOTES

Acts 5:29 Then Peter and the other apostles answered and said, We ought to obey God rather than men.

Job 32:11 Behold, I waited for your words; I gave ear to your reasons, whilst ye searched out what to say.

Romans 11:29 For the gifts and calling of God are without repentance.

2 Peter 1:10 Wherefore the rather, brethren, give diligence to make your calling and election sure: for if ye do these things, ye shall never fall:

Romans 3:4 God forbid: yea, let God be true, but every man a liar; as it is written, That thou mightest be justified in thy sayings, and mightest overcome when thou art judged.

Acts 17:11 These were more noble than those in Thessalonica, in that they received the word with all readiness of mind, **and searched the scriptures daily, whether those things were so.**

1 Corinthians 10:15 I speak as to wise men; judge ye what I say.

John 7:24 Judge not according to the appearance, but judge righteous judgment.

1 Corinthians 2:15 But he that is spiritual judgeth all things, yet he himself is judged of no man.

Matthew 23:23 Woe unto you, scribes and Pharisees, hypocrites! for ye pay tithe of mint and anise and cummin, and have omitted the weightier matters of the law, judgment, mercy, and faith: these ought ye to have done, and not to leave the other undone.

Part Three
Approaching Adventure

§

Dedicated to Reverend Charles Steele
January 8, 1937- December 6, 2011

Everyone knows death is coming. Christians possess the joyful belief of life beyond the grave; however, when the death a doctor is talking about is your own, personal faith cries out for understanding. The impending great adventure provokes our faith in ways that living cannot do. The irony is profound.

So Chuck, this Bible study is for you. For over 30 years you have been my friend and mentor. And now, it appears you are going to heaven before me; although one never knows. The appointed time for going to heaven is entirely up to God. As heaven draws closer to us all, I know more deeply than ever this world does not belong to us, not in its present spiritual shape anyway. Quite frankly there's not enough time for us here; there is not supposed to be.

Your Friend and fellow Bible Student,
Joseph Dulmage, August 7, 2011

Heaven

§

MANY PEOPLE THINK ABOUT HEAVEN in abstract imaginative ways; they consider it a spiritual, nearly incomprehensible dimension. But God made heaven a real place, physical tangible real estate. Heaven is comprehensible; God tells us many things about heaven. *1ˢᵗ Corinthians 2:9*, frequently quoted to establish what we cannot know; yet the very next verse says God reveals truths to believers.

> *1 Corinthians 2:9-10 But as it is written, Eye hath not seen, nor ear heard, neither have entered into the heart of man, the things which God hath prepared for them that love him. 10 But God hath revealed them unto us by his Spirit: for the Spirit searcheth all things, yea, the deep things of God.*

While heaven is certainly a place saved souls go after bodies die, heaven is far more than some surreal, spiritual dimension. Don't forget God furnishes our souls with new physical bodies- which engage in physical activities. Once in heaven we will, no doubt, want to sit down now and then; why not on a nice chair? Thinking about heaven in this way makes it easier to understand. In other words, heaven is a physical place where you could travel if you made the necessary preparations, much like taking a long journey to another country here on earth.

Think about Adam and Eve living in the Garden of Eden. Prior to the fall, the earth existed as paradise. Trees grew, flowers bloomed, and mankind lived in harmony with God and nature. Earth's conditions were quite heavenly; expressing this in precise scientific terms, God literally created earth a planet in heaven.

After the Fall, the earth changed drastically. Our planet's condition transformed into something quite different than originally designed, a terrible metamorphosis ensued. Heaven as a whole did not change, but planet earth went through an enormous transformation. Parts of heaven surrounding earth (solar system) also greatly changed. No longer was earth a perfect place where people live in harmony with God. Since physical death became a fact of life, the idea of heaven being a place one goes after death came into existence.

Christians actually know more about heaven than they realize. That may sound like an odd statement, but if you believe in Jesus 2nd Coming, you know a great deal about heaven.

For the last 2,000 years God has added souls to his Church. One day Jesus gathers all Christians who ever lived to one location in the 3rd heaven. The final generation of Christians never dies physically, they receive immortal bodies and taken to heaven in an instant. This tremendous supernatural event is the Rapture.

1 Thessalonians 4:16-18 For the Lord himself shall descend from heaven with a shout, with the voice of the archangel, and with the trump of God: and the dead in Christ shall rise first: 17 Then we which are alive and remain shall be caught up together with them in the clouds, to meet the Lord in the air: and so shall we ever be with the Lord. 18 Wherefore comfort one another with these words.

1 Corinthians 15:51-52 Behold, I shew you a mystery; We shall not all sleep, but we shall all be changed, 52 In a moment, in the twinkling of an eye, at the last trump: for the trumpet shall sound, and the dead shall be raised incorruptible, and we shall be changed.

Soon after the Rapture, Christians return to earth with Jesus Christ at his 2nd Coming. Then an age begins we call the Millennium. The Millennium is literally the first 1,000 years of heaven. God does not re-create heaven and earth until after the Millennium is over; therefore Christians return to the same earth they just left a few years earlier. The earth's geography remains largely unaltered. Mountains, oceans, seas, and rivers exist as they do today (2011 AD). Of course last days' wars and tribulation affect landscapes in various ways, but this old earth continues in basically the same condition. This means Christians visiting their favorite beach, park, lakes, and mountains, perhaps even towns -will find them quite familiar. So to the question: What will heaven look like? Answer: Look around you.

God Defines Heaven.

The word **heaven** is in the Bible 552 times, 314 times in the Old Testament; 238 times in the New Testament. The word in plural form *heavens* is in the Bible 130 times, 110 in the Old Testament; 20 in the New Testament.

God's first creative act makes heaven and earth. Observe God speaks about heaven in very physical and scientific terms. God makes the firmament (the space where the, moon, planets, Sun and stars exist) God defines Heaven as the firmament itself.

> ***Genesis 1:1*** *In the beginning God created the heaven and the earth.*

Heaven is the universe. Earth is in Heaven.

> ***Genesis 1:7-8*** *And God made the firmament, and divided the waters which were under the firmament from the waters which were above the firmament: and it was so.* ***8 And God called the firmament Heaven.*** *And the evening and the morning were the second day.*

Genesis 1:14-17 And God said, Let there be lights in the firmament of the heaven to divide the day from the night; and let them be for signs, and for seasons, and for days, and years: 15 And let them be for lights in the firmament of the heaven to give light upon the earth: and it was so. 16 And God made two great lights; the greater light to rule the day, and the lesser light to rule the night: he made the stars also. 17 And God set them in the firmament of the heaven to give light upon the earth,

FIRMAMENT, UNIVERSE, COSMOS, SPACE

When we think about the shapes of countries, we call it geography. When we think about the shape of the universe, we call it cosmography. Just as geographic locations on earth differ from one another, regions within the universe (Heaven) exist in vastly different conditions. Presently, some parts of the universe exist in a wonderful (heavenly) condition and other parts of the universe exist in terrible (cursed) condition.

Cosmography - the science mapping the general features of the universe; describes both heaven and earth; the sciences involved in the study of the physical world and its phenomena; a general description of the universe.

Read *Genesis 1:2-7* while considering the following analogy:

Originally, (Genesis 1:1), one uninterrupted, infinite expanse of space, notice heaven is singular. By verse two, however, God renders earth void and darkness is everywhere, and heaven fills with water. This water is called the deep. God separates the waters and the firmament appears. We can understand the physical characteristics of heaven by outlining or mapping just as one might draw the coastline of a country.

Imagine a basketball submerged deep into the ocean. Miles of water surround the ball on every side. Now imagine the basketball has infinite elasticity, and God begins pumping air into the ball. As the basketball enlarges it separates (pushes back) the deep water on every side. When the expansion stops the water remains above the rim of the basketball. The space inside the basketball is the firmament (heaven). And in this space God puts the stars, planets, sun, and the moon. After God separates the water, Heaven is divided into three compartments. This is why the Bible often refers to heaven in plural form. God's dwelling place is in the third heaven. The third heaven contains an eternal city called Mount Zion, City on the sides of the North, or Heaven's Jerusalem. Within that city is a temple, and within the temple is a throne.

Gen. 1:2 And the earth was without form, and void; and darkness was upon the face of the deep. And the Spirit of God moved upon the face of the waters.

Genesis 1:6-8 And God said, Let there be a firmament in the midst of the waters, and let it divide the waters from the waters. 7 And God made the firmament, and divided the waters which were under the firmament from the waters which were above the firmament: and it was so. 8 And God called the firmament Heaven. And the evening and the morning were the second day.

1. The 1st heaven contains the earth. Earth is surrounded by the 1st heaven, our atmosphere.
2. The 2nd heaven contains the moon, planets, all the stars and galaxies. Where earth's atmosphere ends, the 2nd heaven begins (about 120 miles above earth).
3. Water (called the deep) surrounds the 2nd heaven. The deep is literally a barrier separating the 2nd and the 3rd heaven. For sake of illustration: If one were to travel in a spaceship in any direction from the earth, one would eventually hit water (in billions of light years).
4. The 3rd heaven begins where the deep ends. The 3rd heaven exists above the deep. The 3rd heaven is infinite; it is where God's eternal city and temple are located.

Verses depicting 3 heavens, and the water between the 2ⁿᵈ and 3ʳᵈ heaven.

Deuteronomy 10:14 Behold, the heaven and the heaven of heavens is the LORD'S thy God, the earth also, with all that therein is.

*Psalms 148:1-4 Praise ye the LORD. Praise ye the LORD from the heavens: praise him in the heights. 2 Praise ye him, all his angels: praise ye him, all his hosts. 3 Praise ye him, sun and moon: praise him, all ye stars of light. 4 **Praise him, ye heavens of heavens, and ye waters that be above the heavens.***

*2 Corinthians 12:2 I knew a man in Christ above fourteen years ago, (whether in the body, I cannot tell; or whether out of the body, I cannot tell: God knoweth;) such an one caught up to the **third heaven**.*

Thought to ponder: It is interesting to examine the construction of the word universe. **Uni** and **verse,** uni- meaning one- and verse meaning text. God made everything in one verse, hence we have the uni-verse; therefore, when scientists refer to the cosmos as the universe, they are unconsciously referring to *Genesis 1:1.*

Chapter Notes

Psalms 11:4 The LORD is in his holy temple, the LORD'S throne is in heaven: his eyes behold, his eyelids try, the children of men.

Revelation 11:19 And the temple of God was opened in heaven, and there was seen in his temple the ark of his testament: and there were lightnings, and voices, and thunderings, and an earthquake, and great hail.

2 Chronicles 6:39 *Then hear thou from the heavens, even from thy dwelling place, their prayer and their supplications, and maintain their cause, and forgive thy people which have sinned against thee.*

Psalms 48:2 *Beautiful for situation, the joy of the whole earth, is mount Zion, on the sides of the north, the city of the great King.*

Ephesians 4:10 *He that descended is the same also that ascended up far above all heavens, that he might fill all things.)*

Psalms 48:2 *Beautiful for situation, the joy of the whole earth, is mount Zion, on the sides of the north, the city of the great King.*

Isaiah 14:13 *For thou hast said in thine heart, I will ascend into heaven, I will exalt my throne above the stars of God: I will sit also upon the mount of the congregation, in the sides of the north:*

Psalms 19:1-2 *To the chief Musician, A Psalm of David. The heavens declare the glory of God; and the firmament sheweth his handywork.* **2 Day unto day uttereth speech, and night unto night sheweth knowledge.**

Psalms 8:1-4 *To the chief Musician upon Gittith, A Psalm of David. O LORD our Lord, how excellent is thy name in all the earth! who hast set thy glory above the heavens. 2 Out of the mouth of babes and sucklings hast thou ordained strength because of thine enemies, that thou mightest still the enemy and the avenger. 3* **When I consider thy heavens, the work of thy fingers, the moon and the stars,** *which thou hast ordained; 4 What is man, that thou art mindful of him? and the son of man, that thou visitest him?*

Kingdom of Heaven

§

Matthew 6:10 Thy kingdom come. Thy will be done in earth, as it is in heaven.

UNDERSTANDING THE BIG PICTURE

God is building a kingdom. The Bible tells the story of the kingdom's past, present, and future. Just like the cover of a book encloses each individual page, the concept of God building a kingdom encloses every truth in scripture, from the creation of Adam and Eve, to the future creation of a new heaven and a new earth, from the deity of Jesus Christ to Lucifer's damnation. God's kingdom includes heaven, hell, angels, men, women, Israel, the Church, and anything else in existence. Looking at God's program from this perspective, one sees a constant logical plan steadfastly moving toward completion.

THIS HYPOTHESIS MAKES SENSE OF HUMAN HISTORY

Men forming governments is also the story of human history. A kingdom is merely a particular form of government. Some countries rule with kings or dictators; other countries rule via democracies, republics, or oligarchies. Of course, the world tries to do it without God, but never the less, people always try to build a kingdom. Whether a primitive tribe fights another tribe for better hunting ground, or a mighty nation battles another nation over land boundaries or religion, the ultimate motive attempts to make a better, more fulfilling government. A better kingdom inspired the great philosophic thinkers. Inevitably, political leaders emerge representing various ideas how to accomplish their goals. Communism and capitalism represent two hugely opposing views, but both endeavor to construct better governments. Mankind's continuing quest strives to build the world's best kingdom?

The Bible can be viewed as a huge kingdom building political campaign.

Psalms 22:28 *For the kingdom is the LORD'S: and he is the governor among the nations.*

GOD'S KINGDOM

GOD'S KINGDOM IS A THEOCRACY. In other words, God establishes a perfect government with himself ruling as king. Nearly all the prophets, in some way or another, forecast this government. Isaiah sets forth a particularly clear declaration. The scripture below is the greatest political campaign promise ever stated.

> *Isa 9:6-7 For unto us a child is born, unto us a son is given: and the government shall be upon his shoulder: and his name shall be called Wonderful, Counsellor, The mighty God, The everlasting Father, The Prince of Peace. 7 **Of the increase of his government and peace there shall be no end, upon the throne** of David, and upon his kingdom, to order it, and to establish it with judgment and with justice from henceforth even for ever. The zeal of the LORD of hosts will perform this.*

Isaiah (speaking around 700 BC) informs the world a child will be born. As an adult the whole world's government resides on his shoulders. Isaiah tells us the child is God Himself who rules with judgment, justice, and peace; the child is Jesus Christ. God establishes the government on the throne of David. This means the government of Israel is paramount in heaven; it subsumes the entire world and then expands into the universe. Of course, Isaiah speaks of a righteous Israel ruled by God, not the current government existing in the Middle East. An extremely important point is to understand the size of God's Kingdom increases forever. This means the vast majority of people who eventually populate heaven have not even been born.

Comparing Isaiah's prophecy to original plans for Adam and Eve, we see profound similarities. God created the first man and woman and ordered them to populate the earth. Indeed, Adam and Eve were the first human rulers of the kingdom. Looking at God's intention for the first human beings manifests God intentions for the future. In Adam's age of innocence, the spirit world and physical world jelled together. Can you imagine a better heaven than Adam's and Eve's world before the Fall? A sublime existence, no death, pain, or sorrow-God even selected one's perfect spouse! And with continued child birth, God planned to populate the universe. God's plans remain the same; he has not changed his mind.

Isaiah 45:18 For thus saith the LORD that created the heavens; God himself that formed the earth and made it; he hath established it, he created it not in vain, he formed it to be inhabited: I am the LORD; and there is none else.

Genesis 1:28 And God blessed them, and God said unto them, Be fruitful, and multiply, and replenish the earth, and subdue it: and have dominion over the fish of the sea, and over the fowl of the air, and over every living thing that moveth upon the earth.

Israel

One nation under God

GOD'S RELATIONSHIP WITH ISRAEL IS one of the Bible's great mysteries. Israel may be viewed as a prototype of the kingdom. *A prototype is an original model on which the coming final product is built.* The kingdom of heaven's capital is Jerusalem. (See chapter Jerusalem) And the kingdom's managers and leaders will be Jewish. This explains why Satan periodically influences world leaders like Pharaoh, Ahasuerus, Hitler, and scores of others to try and exterminate the Jew. Antisemitism is easily explained. In theory, if Satan annihilates the Jew, he stops God's kingdom from coming. But, of course, nothing can stop God's absolute plan. Even before Israel existed, God ordained his kingdom according to his predestinated plan for Israel.

> **Deuteronomy 32:8** *When the Most High divided to the nations their inheritance, when he separated the sons of Adam, he set the bounds of the people according to the number of the children of Israel.*

God's Kingdom includes two major human components, the Church and Israel. Both groups enjoy citizenship in God's kingdom. But just as differences exist between the Kingdom of God and the Kingdom of Heaven, we must also differentiate between Israel and the Church.

Romans 11:25 *For I would not, brethren, **that ye should be ignorant of this mystery,** lest ye should be wise in your own conceits; that blindness in part is happened to Israel, until the fulness of the Gentiles be come in.*

Israel is 2,000 years older than the Church. Israel is a physical nation as opposed to a spiritual entity. Unlike the Church, one cannot join Israel by believing in Jesus Christ. To be an Israelite one must be physically born an Israelite. The only exceptions are approved marriages, when a gentile woman marries a male Israeli. In rare cases a legal adoption is accepted. Understand however- being a citizen of Israel does not automatically make one a citizen in God's future kingdom. For an individual to be saved, faith in Jesus Christ is necessary. In other words, being a citizen of Israel does not guarantee one goes to heaven.

Israel and Outer Space

§

THE NATION ISRAEL CONTINUES TO increase in size forever and ever. Unlike the Church, Israel's population is infinite. Consider the promise given to Abraham some 4,000 years ago concerning population increase. These prophecies coincide perfectly with Isaiah 9:7, *of the increase of his government and peace there shall be no end...*

> **Genesis 15:5** *And he brought him forth abroad, and said, Look now toward heaven, and tell the stars, if thou be able to number them: and he said unto him, So shall thy seed be.*

> **Gen 22:17** *That in blessing I will bless thee, and in multiplying I will multiply thy seed as the stars of the heaven, and as the sand which is upon the sea shore; and thy seed shall possess the gate of his enemies;*

> **Isa 9:7** *Of the increase of his government and peace there shall be no end, upon the throne of David, and upon his kingdom, to order it, and to establish it with judgment and with justice from henceforth even for ever. The zeal of the LORD of hosts will perform this.*

To be numbered as the stars and the sands of the sea demand more room than the earth can hold. When Abraham looked toward heaven, he viewed the kingdom of heaven's destiny. The Jew will populate heaven. In the future, a huge difference between Israel and the Church is men and women in Israel continue getting married and having children, whereas men and women in the Church do not reproduce.

> *1 Chronicles 27:23 But David took not the number of them from twenty years old and under: because the LORD had said he would increase Israel like to the stars of the heavens.*

KING DAVID'S SEED AND THE LEVITES PROMISED INFINITY REPRODUCTION.

> *Jeremiah 33:22 As the host of heaven cannot be numbered, neither the sand of the sea measured: so will I multiply the seed of David my servant, and the Levites that minister unto me.*

THOUGHT TO PONDER

An estimated number of the grains of sand on earth: 7.5 x 10^{18} grains of sand, or seven quintillion, five hundred quadrillion grains. The stars in heaven number higher, much higher.

No other nation is given this promise of expansion. Israel stumbled much on her journey to the stars, but her backsliding is only temporary. In righteous anger, God scattered the Jew among all nations, but He has not cast away his people or withdrawn his promises.

> *Zechariah 7:14 But I scattered them with a whirlwind among all the nations whom they knew not. Thus the land was desolate after them, that no man passed through nor returned: for they laid the pleasant land desolate..*

> *Amos 9:9 For, lo, I will command, and I will sift the house of Israel among all nations, like as corn is sifted in a sieve, yet shall not the least grain Fall upon the earth.*

Ironically, the Jewish Diaspora is the key for interpreting the Gentiles' future. God is no respecter of persons, but he is a respecter of a nation, and Israel is a nation formed and shaped by God. Indeed, the future is written and settled. All Gentile nations end. The word of God sets in order the things to come.

> *Jeremiah 46:28* *Fear thou not, O Jacob my servant, saith the LORD: for I am with thee;* ***for I will make a full end of all the nations whither I have driven thee**: but I will not make a full end of thee, but correct thee in measure; yet will I not leave thee wholly unpunished.*

> *Jeremiah 30:11* *For I am with thee, saith the LORD, to save thee:* ***though I make a full end of all nations whither I have scattered thee, yet will I not make a full end of thee:** but I will correct thee in measure, and will not leave thee altogether unpunished.*

> *Isaiah 40:17* *All nations before him are as nothing; and they are counted to him less than nothing, and vanity.*

Gentile nations continue to exist even beyond the Millennium walking in the light of New Jerusalem *Rev. 21:23-24*, but this does not alter the prophecies. Gentile nations come to an end in the distant future. For wherever God scattered the Jew (and the scattering was to all nations) that nation ends. Israel absorbs saved gentile nations.

During the Millennium, Gentiles receive their blessings through the Jew, and Israel becomes an absolute hegemony. Gentile nations submitted to Israel's authority are subsumed in the Abrahamic covenant. They receive inheritance with Israel and assigned a tribe. Nations that do not submit to Israel face destruction. If all this sounds disturbing remember, at this time, Jesus Christ is ruling Israel; therefore, Israelites are servants and ambassadors for God. Refusing Israel, is the equivalent of refusing Jesus Christ.

Isaiah 60:12 For the nation and kingdom that will not serve thee shall perish; yea, those nations shall be utterly wasted.

Zechariah 8:22-23 Yea, many people and strong nations shall come to seek the LORD of hosts in Jerusalem, and to pray before the LORD. 23 Thus saith the LORD of hosts; In those days it shall come to pass, that ten men shall take hold out of all languages of the nations, even shall take hold of the skirt of him that is a Jew, saying, We will go with you: for we have heard that God is with you.

Genesis 12:2-3 And I will make of thee a great nation, and I will bless thee, and make thy name great; and thou shalt be a blessing: 3 And I will bless them that bless thee, and curse him that curseth thee: and in thee shall all families of the earth be blessed.

Even today Jews are natural born leaders; however, without Jesus Christ they lose their effectiveness and their abilities diminish greatly. The doctrinal application for the passage below is for Israel. Christians often misapply these verses to the Church. One may apply the passages to the Church in a spiritual or moral sense, but the doctrinal fact remains- Jesus said this to Israel who was largely rejecting him. Jews are the salt of the earth, not Christians.

Matthew 5:13-14 13 Ye are the salt of the earth: but if the salt have lost his savour, wherewith shall it be salted? it is thenceforth good for nothing, but to be cast out, and to be trodden under foot of men. 14 Ye are the light of the world. A city that is set on an hill cannot be hid.

Read Moses' address in Deuteronomy 29 carefully. Ponder the prophetic weight. Give scrutiny to the stranger who receives covenant promises verse 15. Those who are *not here with us this day* are future saved Gentiles.

Deuteronomy 29:10-15 *Ye stand this day all of you before the LORD your God; your captains of your tribes, your elders, and your officers, with all the men of Israel,* ***11*** *Your little ones, your wives, and thy stranger that is in thy camp, from the hewer of thy wood unto the drawer of thy water:* ***12*** *That thou shouldest enter into covenant with the LORD thy God, and into his oath, which the LORD thy God maketh with thee this day:* ***13*** *That he may establish thee to day for a people unto himself, and that he may be unto thee a God, as he hath said unto thee, and as he hath sworn unto thy fathers, to Abraham, to Isaac, and to Jacob.* ***14*** *Neither with you only do I make this covenant and this oath;* ***15 But with him that standeth here with us this day before the LORD our God, and also with him that is not here with us this day:***

ISRAEL SUBSUMES ALL SAVED GENTILES

Do not confuse this program with the mission of the Christian Church; the Church does not increase her numbers via physical childbirth. But even the Church; the Gentile Bride of Jesus Christ, becomes Jewish. Israel's history forecasts the future; God's purpose and intent remains steadfast. Approved Gentile women who married Hebrews were absorbed by Israel and considered Jews. For example Rebecca, Leah, Rachel, Ruth, Bathsheba -all Gentiles who became legally Jewish by marriage; and assimilated into their husband's tribe. When Christians marry the Lord Jesus at a legal wedding- Israel subsumes them. All Christians become members of the tribe of Judah.

The absorption of Gentiles into specific Israeli tribe takes place at the end of the Millennium. More accurately, the legal designation and/or assigning of tribes happen at that time. Ultimately, every saved human being becomes Jewish! An exception to this process is the Christian Church (Jesus' Bride) Christians officially become part of Israel at their wedding which takes place in heaven just prior to the 2nd Advent.

Prophet Ezekiel deals with Gentiles in more detail. Tremendous information on the Millennium Kingdom of heaven in Chapters 40-48. The millennium prophecy below provides more evidence for Israel subsuming Gentiles. The strangers are Gentiles.

*Ezekiel 47:21-23 So shall ye divide this land unto you according to the tribes of Israel. 22 And it shall come to pass, that ye shall divide it by lot for an inheritance unto you, and **to the strangers that sojourn among you,** which shall beget children among you: and they shall be unto you as born in the country among the children of Israel; they shall have inheritance with you among the tribes of Israel. 23 And it shall come to pass, that in what tribe the stranger sojourneth, there shall ye give him his inheritance, saith the Lord GOD.*

*Isaiah 54:3 For thou shalt break forth on the right hand and on the left; **and thy seed shall inherit the Gentiles,** and make the desolate cities to be inhabited.*

Zechariah 2:11-13 And many nations shall be joined to the LORD in that day, and shall be my people: and I will dwell in the midst of thee, and thou shalt know that the LORD of hosts hath sent me unto thee. 12 And the LORD shall inherit Judah his portion in the holy land, and shall choose Jerusalem again. 13 Be silent, O all flesh, before the LORD: for he is raised up out of his holy habitation.

*Dan 2:44 And in the days of these kings shall the God of heaven set up a kingdom, which shall never be destroyed: and the kingdom shall not be left to other people, **but it shall break in pieces and consume all these kingdoms,** and it shall stand for ever.*

*Isaiah 14:1 For the LORD will have mercy on Jacob, and will yet choose Israel, and set them in their own land: **and the strangers***

**shall be joined with them, and they shall cleave to the house
of Jacob.**

Num 15:15 *One ordinance shall be both for you of the congregation, and also for the stranger that sojourneth with you, an ordinance for ever in your generations: as ye are, so shall the stranger
be before the LORD.*

Isa 26:15 *Thou hast increased the nation, O LORD, thou hast
increased the nation: thou art glorified: thou hadst removed it far
unto all the ends of the earth.*

Jeremiah 30:11 *For I am with thee, saith the LORD, to save thee:*
**though I make a full end of all nations whither I have scat-
tered thee, yet will I not make a full end of thee:** *but I will correct thee in measure, and will not leave thee altogether unpunished.*

Genesis 12:1-3 *Now the LORD had said unto Abram, Get thee
out of thy country, and from thy kindred, and from thy father's
house, unto a land that I will shew thee: 2 And I will make of thee
a great nation, and I will bless thee, and make thy name great;
and thou shalt be a blessing: 3 And I will bless them that bless thee,
and curse him that curseth thee: and in thee shall all families of the
earth be blessed.*

Heaven's Government.

ALL NATIONS EMPLOY GOVERNING MECHANISMS to make laws and provide for societal needs. Just as organizational structures exist for this world's nations, so also for God's kingdom. To help understand how the kingdom operates, an analogy contrasts a national government to the future kingdom of heaven. No matter the country one lives, the analogy should easily adapt to any particular government. Since the author is an American, America's republic is used.

In 2011 AD, America operates with a President overseeing the executive branch- the Senate and Congress serve as congressional branch- and the Supreme Court as the judicial branch. Together these three branches provide the means for running America. The nation has a capital city, Washington DC, where these organizations are located.

The Kingdom of Heaven also has a capital city. Jerusalem serves as the Washington DC for the Kingdom of Heaven. The primary capital building is the temple (made by God). The temple houses God's throne.

In the future, Jerusalem is earth's capital city, Jerusalem is also the capital of the universe, the exact place where God puts his temple and his throne. Jesus Christ rules the entire universe from Jerusalem. Remember, *Isaiah 9:7* told us the government increases in size forever. Earth, then, is only the beginning. Eventually, God plans on populating outer space with human beings.

Notice God actually transplants geography and architecture from the 3rd heaven and places them in Israel.

> *Ezekiel 43:7 And he said unto me, Son of man, the place of my throne, and the place of the soles of my feet, **where I will dwell in the midst of the children of Israel for ever,** and my holy name, shall the house of Israel no more defile, neither they, nor their kings, by their whoredom, nor by the carcases of their kings in their high places.*

> *Ezekiel 37:26-28 Moreover I will make a covenant of peace with them; it shall be an everlasting covenant with them: and I will place them, and multiply them, **and will set my sanctuary in the midst of them for evermore. 27 My tabernacle also shall be with them:** yea, I will be their God, and they shall be my people. 28 And the heathen shall know that I the LORD do sanctify Israel, when my sanctuary shall be in the midst of them for evermore.*

> *Isaiah 2:1-5 The word that Isaiah the son of Amoz saw concerning Judah and Jerusalem. 2 And it shall come to pass in the last days, that the mountain of the LORD'S house shall be established in the top of the mountains, and shall be exalted above the hills; **and all nations shall flow unto it.** 3 And many people shall go and say, Come ye, and let us go up to the mountain of the LORD, to the house of the God of Jacob; and he will teach us of his ways, and we will walk in his paths: for out of Zion shall go forth the law, and the word of the LORD from Jerusalem. 4 And he shall judge among the nations, and shall rebuke many people: and they shall beat their swords into plowshares, and their spears into pruninghooks: nation shall not lift up sword against nation, neither shall they learn war any more. 5 O house of Jacob, come ye, and let us walk in the light of the LORD.*

God's kingdom is on a Jewish platform, but a Jewish platform that acknowledges Jesus Christ as Messiah. Jesus Christ rules from Jerusalem as a dictator king. But remember, Jesus is King of kings;

there are rulers beneath him. The Kingdom of Heaven's highest-ranking king under Jesus Christ is King David. Prophets wrote the promises hundreds of years after David died.

Jeremiah 30:9 But they shall serve the LORD their God, and David their king, whom I will raise up unto them.

> *Ezekiel 37:22-24 And I will make them one nation in the land upon the mountains of Israel; and one king shall be king to them all: and they shall be no more two nations, neither shall they be divided into two kingdoms any more at all: 23 Neither shall they defile themselves any more with their idols, nor with their detestable things, nor with any of their transgressions: but I will save them out of all their dwellingplaces, wherein they have sinned, and will cleanse them: so shall they be my people, **and I will be their God. 24 And David my servant shall be king over them; and they all shall have one shepherd: they shall also walk in my judgments, and observe my statutes, and do them.***

When Ezekiel wrote the above prophecy, David had been dead for several hundred years. The passage concerns the future. God resurrects David to be Israel's prince and rule forever.

> *Ezekiel 37:25-28 And they shall dwell in the land that I have given unto Jacob my servant, wherein your fathers have dwelt; and they shall dwell therein, even they, and their children, and their children's children for ever: **and my servant David shall be their prince for ever.** 26 Moreover I will make a covenant of peace with them; it shall be an everlasting covenant with them: and I will place them, and multiply them, and will set my sanctuary in the midst of them for evermore. 27 My tabernacle also shall be with them: yea, I will be their God, and they shall be my people. 28 And the heathen shall know that I the LORD do sanctify Israel, when my sanctuary shall be in the midst of them for evermore.*

Making Laws

ANALOGOUS COMMENTARY FOR CONGRESSIONAL LEGISLATION is easy. Since Jesus rules Heaven as supreme King- no governmental body makes laws. All laws are authorized by King Jesus Christ. No one votes in this arrangement. Individuals do have a choice to make:

1. Become a citizen in Christ's kingdom by making Jesus Christ their King.
2. Choose not to be a citizen.

Judicial Branch

§

FASCINATINGLY, JUDGES EXIST TO HELP with questions about God's laws. These judges also help govern the nation, which eventually extends to the entire universe. In the book of Judges, the Bible gives information on God's governing intentions. God raised up judges to help with certain national crisis. But overall judges had limited power.

> *Judges 2:16-19 Nevertheless the LORD raised up judges, which delivered them out of the hand of those that spoiled them. 17 And yet they would not hearken unto their judges, but they went a whoring after other gods, and bowed themselves unto them: they turned quickly out of the way which their fathers walked in, obeying the commandments of the LORD; but they did not so. 18 And when the LORD raised them up judges, then the LORD was with the judge, and delivered them out of the hand of their enemies all the days of the judge: for it repented the LORD because of their groanings by reason of them that oppressed them and vexed them. 19 And it came to pass, when the judge was dead, that they returned, and corrupted themselves more than their fathers, in following other gods to serve them, and to bow down unto them; they ceased not from their own doings, nor from their stubborn way.*

God never intended to rule Israel with a human king. In fact, he tried to talk Israel out of it when they asked for a king. God wanted to govern through limited authority via judges. It seems God believes in freedom for his people. Or in other words- the least government is the best government. Nevertheless- stubborn human wills insisted- and God allowed a king. Read and ponder the passage below. This passage provides significant insight into God's governing ideology. Choosing a human king was a major turning point in Israel's history.

So Israel gets their way, and the Bible records another example of God respecting human authority. This development illuminates God's relationship with mankind. Our freewill can make decisions that have significant consequences. Some decisions create eternal ramifications. Even though God discouraged Israel from having a human king, he accepted their decision. After God declares in writing what is best for men, he lets men have their way, and then God incorporates the decision into his eternal destiny. We have already seen King David receives a throne in eternity. Truly God's relationship to man is ponderous.

*1 Samuel 8:4-22 Then all the elders of Israel gathered themselves together, and came to Samuel unto Ramah, 5 And said unto him, Behold, thou art old, and thy sons walk not in thy ways: now make us a king to judge us like all the nations. **6 But the thing displeased Samuel, when they said, Give us a king to judge us. And Samuel prayed unto the LORD. 7 And the LORD said unto Samuel, Hearken unto the voice of the people in all that they say unto thee: for they have not rejected thee, but they have rejected me, that I should not reign over them.** 8 According to all the works which they have done since the day that I brought them up out of Egypt even unto this day, wherewith they have forsaken me, and served other gods, so do they also unto thee. **9 Now therefore hearken unto their voice: howbeit yet protest solemnly unto them,** and shew them the manner of the king that shall reign over them. 10 And Samuel told all the words of the LORD unto the people that asked of him a king. 11 And he said, This will be the manner of the king that shall reign over you: He will take your sons, and appoint* *them for himself, for his chariots, and to be his horsemen; and some shall run before his chariots. 12 And he will appoint him captains over thousands, and captains over fifties; and will set them to ear his ground, and to reap his harvest, and to make his instruments of war, and instruments of his chariots. 13 And he will take your daughters to be confectionaries, and to be cooks, and to be bakers. 14 And he will take your fields, and your vineyards, and your oliveyards, even the best of them, and give them to his servants. 15 And he will take the tenth of your seed, and of your vineyards, and give to his officers, and to his servants. 16 And he will take your menservants, and your maidservants, and your goodliest young men, and your asses, and put them to his work. 17 He will take the tenth of your sheep: and ye shall be his servants. 18 And ye shall cry out in that day because of your king which ye shall have chosen you; and the LORD will not hear you in that day. 19 Nevertheless the people refused to obey the voice of Samuel; and they said, Nay; but we will have a king over us; 20 That we also may be like all the nations; and that our king may judge us, and go out before us, and fight our battles. 21 And Samuel heard all the words of the people, and he rehearsed them in the ears of the LORD. 22 And the LORD said to Samuel, Hearken unto their voice, and make them a king. And Samuel said unto the men of Israel, Go ye every man unto his city.*

Psalms 8:3-6 *When I consider thy heavens, the work of thy fingers, the moon and the stars, which thou hast ordained; 4 What is man, that thou art mindful of him? and the son of man, that thou visitest him? 5 For thou hast made him a little lower than the angels, and hast crowned him with glory and honour. 6 Thou madest him to have dominion over the works of thy hands; thou hast put all things under his feet:*

Job 7:17 *What is man, that thou shouldest magnify him? and that thou shouldest set thine heart upon him?*

Future Judges

WITH ALL THE HISTORY AND developments under kings, it would be easy to forget about judges, but then Isaiah informs Israel he plans to restore judges in his coming kingdom. Calling Jerusalem the *city of righteousness* and the *faithful city* identifies the age as the Millennium. 700 years after Isaiah's prophecy, Jesus identifies those judges. When the apostles ask about their future, Jesus informs them they rule as judges in the age to come. *Luke 22:28-30* Imagine knowing exactly your assigned job in heaven! After this revelation, no doubt the apostles spent several evenings studying the books of Judges, and 1st and 2nd Samuel. Just before Jesus left earth, the apostles wondered when the kingdom gets set up; they anticipated with great excitement their new positions.

*Isaiah 1:25-27 And I will turn my hand upon thee, and purely purge away thy dross, and take away all thy tin: **26 And I will restore thy judges as at the first,** and thy counsellers as at the beginning: afterward thou shalt be called, The city of righteousness, the faithful city. 27 Zion shall be redeemed with judgment, and her converts with righteousness.*

Luke 22:28-30 Ye are they which have continued with me in my temptations. 29 And I appoint unto you a kingdom, as my Father hath appointed unto me; 30 That ye may eat and drink at my table in my kingdom, and sit on thrones judging the twelve tribes of Israel.

***Acts 1:6-9** When they therefore were come together, they asked of him, saying, Lord, wilt thou at this time restore again the kingdom to Israel? **7** And he said unto them, It is not for you to know the times or the seasons, which the Father hath put in his own power. **8** But ye shall receive power, after that the Holy Ghost is come upon you: and ye shall be witnesses unto me both in Jerusalem, and in all Judaea, and in Samaria, and unto the uttermost part of the earth. **9** And when he had spoken these things, while they beheld, he was taken up; and a cloud received him out of their sight.* Peter and the apostles were being responsible when they realized they had to replace Judas Iscariot. Since Jesus promised 12 thrones, and now there were only 11 apostles- there was no doubt what the first order of business had to be.

Millennium

Heaven's first 1,000 years

THE BIBLE IDENTIFIES THE MILLENNIUM as the *regeneration.* It
is also called the *kingdom, the rest, and the times of refreshing.*
Considering what the earth has been through, these are well earned
adjectives.

*Matthew 19:27-28 Then answered Peter and said unto him,
Behold, we have forsaken all, and followed thee; what shall we have
therefore? 28 And Jesus said unto them, Verily I say unto you,
That ye which have followed me,* **in the regeneration** *when the
Son of man shall sit in the throne of his glory, ye also shall sit upon
twelve thrones, judging the twelve tribes of Israel.*

*Acts 3:19 Repent ye therefore, and be converted, that your sins may
be blotted out, when the* **times of refreshing** *shall come from the
presence of the Lord;*

Isaiah 28:12 To whom he said, This is **the rest** *wherewith ye may
cause the weary to rest; and this is the refreshing: yet they would
not hear.*

Hebrews 4:9 There remaineth therefore **a rest** *to the people of
God.*

Indeed this old earth, ravished by abuse; requires some serious rest and relaxation. God begins a process of restoration. And as the word regeneration implies, this old earth starts to heal. During the Millennium, God causes tremendous geographic change. God literally re-sculptures the planet, beginning the moment Jesus Christ returns to earth. His feet touch down on Mt. Olivet and a great geographic upheaval begins, the earth opens revealing a huge new valley exposing a large portion of the nether earth. Glorious treasures buried inside will once again be visible and accessible for all God's people. This wondrous opening of the earth is prophesied by Isaiah and Zechariah.

When Jesus touches down on the Mount of Olives, the earth's regeneration begins *Mt. 19:28*. The times of refreshing arrive *Acts 3:19* Israel becomes the head of nations *Ro. 11:12*.

Zechariah 14:4 And his feet shall stand in that day upon the mount of Olives, which is before Jerusalem on the east, and the mount of Olives shall cleave in the midst thereof toward the east and toward the west, and there shall be a very great valley; and half of the mountain shall remove toward the north, and half of it toward the south.

*Isaiah 45:3-8 And I will give thee the treasures of darkness, and hidden riches of secret places, that thou mayest know that I, the LORD, which call thee by thy name, am the God of Israel. 4 For Jacob my servant's sake, and Israel mine elect, I have even called thee by thy name: I have surnamed thee, though thou hast not known me. 5 I am the LORD, and there is none else, there is no God beside me: I girded thee, though thou hast not known me: 6 That they may know from the rising of the sun, and from the west, that there is none beside me. I am the LORD, and there is none else. 7 I form the light, and create darkness: I make peace, and create evil: I the LORD do all these things. 8 **Drop down, ye heavens,***

from above, and let the skies pour down righteousness: let the earth open, *and let them bring forth salvation, and let righteousness spring up together; I the LORD have created it.*

As the geographical regeneration continues; the changes are staggering. At this time God sets Zion and God's Temple in Jerusalem. Quite literally, earthly Jerusalem becomes heaven's Jerusalem. For the capital of the Kingdom of Heaven is once again on earth.

Zechariah 14:9-10 And the LORD shall be king over all the earth: in that day shall there be one LORD, and his name one. **10** *All the land shall be turned as a plain from Geba to Rimmon south of Jerusalem: and it shall be lifted up, and inhabited in her place, from Benjamin's gate unto the place of the first gate, unto the corner gate, and from the tower of Hananeel unto the king's winepresses.*

Isaiah 2:2 And it shall come to pass in the last days, that the mountain of the Lord's house shall be established in the top of the mountains, and shall be exalted above the hills; and all nations shall flow unto it.

Ezek 37:26-27 Moreover I will make a covenant of peace with them; it shall be an everlasting covenant with them: and I will place them, and multiply them, and will set my sanctuary in the midst of them for evermore. 27 My tabernacle also shall be with them: yea, I will be their God, and they shall be my people.

Ezek 43:7 And he said unto me, Son of man, the place of my throne, and the place of the soles of my feet, where I will dwell in the midst of the children of Israel for ever, and my holy name, shall the house of Israel no more defile, neither they, nor their kings, by their whoredom, nor by the carcases of their kings in their high places.

Psalm 48:1-2 A Song and Psalm for the sons of Korah. Great is the LORD, and greatly to be praised in the city of our God, in the mountain of his holiness. 2 Beautiful for situation, the joy of the whole earth, is mount Zion, on the sides of the north, the city of the great King.

Rightly divide the age

Remember, the new earth (and New Jerusalem) are not yet created. After the rapture, Christians live in the 3rd heaven for only a few years Although Christians have incorruptible bodies, and are married to Jesus Christ, they return to earth with Christ at his 2nd Coming. They live on this earth for 1,000 years, before moving to New Jerusalem.

Something to ponder: Jesus returns with his saints from the 3rd heaven, and the earth opens and righteousness comes from below. Think about the statement, *and let them bring forth salvation.* Who is them? What is this salvation and righteousness that spring up? Isaiah's prophecy coincides with *Zechariah 14:4. Isaiah 44:23.*

River of Life

The earth's regeneration is largely a consequence of the river of life emanating from the throne of God. Everywhere the water flows it heals and restores. When the supernatural water touches salt water, the water becomes fresh and fish live abundantly. Along the banks of Zion the tree of life begins to grow in orchards. As one contemplates the river of life, the word regeneration perfectly describes what's happening to the planet.

*Revelation 22:1-3 And he shewed me a pure river of **water of life, clear as crystal, proceeding out of the throne of God and of the Lamb**. 2 In the midst of the street of it, and on either side of the river, was there the tree of life, which bare twelve manner of fruits, and yielded her fruit every month: and the leaves of the tree* *were for the healing of the nations. 3 And there shall be no more curse: but the throne of God and of the Lamb shall be in it; and his servants shall serve him:*

Ezekiel 47:1-11 *Afterward he brought me again unto the door of the house; and,* **behold, waters issued out from under the threshold of the house eastward:** *for the forefront of the house stood toward the east, and the waters came down from under from the right side of the house, at the south side of the altar. 2 Then brought he me out of the way of the gate northward, and led me about the way without unto the utter gate by the way that looketh eastward; and, behold, there ran out waters on the right side. 3 And when the man that had the line in his hand went forth eastward, he measured a thousand cubits, and he brought me through the waters; the waters were to the ancles. 4 Again he measured a thousand, and brought me through the waters; the waters were to the knees. Again he measured a thousand, and brought me through; the waters were to the loins. 5 Afterward he measured a thousand; and it was a river that I could not pass over: for the waters were risen, waters to swim in, a river that could not be passed over. 6 And he said unto me, Son of man, hast thou seen this? Then he brought me, and caused me to return to the brink of the river. 7 Now when I had returned, behold, at the bank of the river were very many trees on the one side and on the other. 8 Then said he unto me, These waters issue out toward the east country, and go down into the desert, and go into the sea: which being brought forth into the sea,* **the waters shall be healed. 9 And it shall come to pass, that every thing that liveth, which moveth, whithersoever the rivers shall come, shall live: and there shall be a very great multitude of fish, because these waters shall come thither: for they shall be healed; and every thing shall live whither the river cometh. 10** *And it shall come to pass, that the fishers shall stand upon it from Engedi even unto Eneglaim;*

they shall be a place to spread forth nets; their fish shall be according to their kinds, as the fish of the great sea, exceeding many. **11** *But the miry places thereof and the marishes thereof shall not be healed; they shall be given to salt..*

Reappearance of Eden; Paradise Found

The Garden of Eden, Paradise, and Abraham's bosom are all the same place. This assertion, of course, needs to be proved with scripture, but for understanding sake, I state my hypothesis now. The Garden of Eden was originally in a valley, and then God covered the valley with land. This means Eden remained where it always was - but now we can't see it because it's buried inside the earth. The earth opening will reveal paradise lost, Eden.

With only casual investigation, the Garden of Eden seems to disappear into obscurity. One could suppose God's curse on the earth simply ravished the garden of God into regular terrain, but several passages indicate God preserved his paradise deep inside the earth.

For illustration; think of the earth as a house, and the ground you're standing on as the roof. Remove the roof and you find several rooms. The most beautiful room is Eden, the paradise of God. The tree of life still exists awaiting its original intention, to provide eternal life to an endless dispensation of God's people yet to be born.

Before Jesus' resurrection, saved souls went to a literal place inside this earth called Abraham's bosom. A place so wonderful God also called it paradise. As Jesus hung on the cross dying for our sins, one of the men crucified with our Lord, put his faith in Christ. Jesus promised he would be in paradise with him that very same day. Jesus calling the place paradise- proves it synonymous with Abraham's bosom.

Luke 23:42-43 And he said unto Jesus, Lord, remember me when thou comest into thy kingdom. 43 And Jesus said unto him, Verily I say unto thee, To day shalt thou be with me in paradise.

Jesus was dead three days. Jesus spent those three days inside the earth. Since the repentant malefactor was with Jesus the same day he died, then they were somewhere inside the earth. Jesus did not ascend into the 3rd heaven until after 3 days. *To day shalt thou be with me in paradise.* That statement, alone, is evidence for paradise being inside the earth.

> **Matthew 12:40** *For as Jonas was three days and three nights in the whale's belly; so shall the Son of man be three days and three nights in the heart of the earth.*

Careful reading of Luke 16 gives a visual perception of the inner earth's geography. Hell and paradise exist side by side inside the earth.

> **Luke 16:20-26** *And there was a certain beggar named Lazarus, which was laid at his gate, full of sores, 21 And desiring to be fed with the crumbs which fell from the rich man's table: moreover the dogs came and licked his sores. 22 And it came to pass, that the beggar died, and was carried by the angels into Abraham's bosom: the rich man also died, and was buried; 23 And in hell he lift up his eyes, being in torments, and seeth Abraham afar off, and Lazarus in his bosom. 24 And he cried and said, Father Abraham, have mercy on me, and send Lazarus, that he may dip the tip of his finger in water, and cool my tongue; for I am tormented in this flame. 25 But Abraham said, Son, remember that thou in thy lifetime receivedst thy good things, and likewise Lazarus evil things: but now he is comforted, and thou art tormented. 26 And beside all this, between us and you there is a great gulf fixed: so that they which would pass from hence to you cannot; neither can they pass to us, that would come from thence.*

PARADISE LOST
The word "paradise is in the Bible three times.

Luke 23:43 And Jesus said unto him, Verily I say unto thee, To day shalt thou be with me in paradise..

2 Corinthians 12:4 How that he was caught up into paradise, and heard unspeakable words, which it is not lawful for a man to utter.

Revelation 2:7 He that hath an ear, let him hear what the Spirit saith unto the churches; To him that overcometh will I give to eat of the tree of life, which is in the midst of the paradise of God.

In 2 Corinthians chapter 12, God takes Apostle Paul to paradise in the third heaven, thus the 3rd heaven also contains a place called paradise. Jesus led captivity captive out of paradise and into the third heaven during his resurrection. Christians believe the captivity to be Old Testament saints temporarily housed in the nether earth paradise. This coincides perfectly with the doctrine of Abraham's bosom and the repentant malefactor who died with Jesus.

Ephesians 4:8-10 Wherefore he saith, When he ascended up on high, he led captivity captive, and gave gifts unto men. 9 (Now that he ascended, what is it but that he also descended first into the lower parts of the earth? 10 He that descended is the same also that ascended up far above all heavens, that he might fill all things.)

Because of that wondrous exodus, many Christians presume paradise is now empty, and God took paradise, itself, to the third heaven. In my opinion, these presumptions go too far. A paradise in heaven is no reason to conclude God removed paradise from earth. Several identically named entities exist simultaneously in heaven and earth

- There is a Jerusalem on earth and a Jerusalem in heaven.
- There was a temple on earth and a temple in heaven.
- There is a Mt. Zion on earth and a Mt. Zion in heaven.
- There is also a paradise in earth and paradise in heaven.

Tree of Life

> *Revelation 2:7 He that hath an ear, let him hear what the Spirit saith unto the churches; To him that overcometh will I give to eat of the tree of life, which is in the midst of the paradise of God.*

Revelation 2:7 provides definitive text. The tree of life exists in the Garden of Eden; thus Eden is paradise. It's really quite reasonable to consider the Garden of Eden as paradise. The tree of life is an earth-based tree. This tree shows up again in the Millennium and in eternity. Always the tree of life is on earth. God intended the tree of life for Adam and Eve and their children to get everlasting physical life, not for the Bride of Jesus Christ (Christians) who receive eternal life at salvation and everlasting physical life at the rapture.

Most churches teach the tree of life is in the 3rd heaven. But this is just one more example of Christians submissively believing theological ideas without investigation. God planted the tree in the Garden of Eden; The Bible never says God transplanted the tree into heavenly Jerusalem.

Thought to ponder: God gives Christians eternal life the instant they are born again; their physical bodies receive immortality at the Rapture. In the future, Israelites and gentiles believe on Jesus Christ, but then they must eat from the tree of life to gain physical immortality.

The end of the Tribulation: Jesus 2ND Advent
The Antichrist gathers the world's armies into one place for the sole purpose of fighting Jesus Christ. As Jesus Christ descends from heaven, the world points their missiles, lazars, guns, and all weapons at him. Hence the world's military welcome for Jesus' 2nd Advent, however, Jesus Christ responds like a Lion, not a Lamb.

Of course the world's military attack accomplishes nothing. Jesus returns triumphantly. The Antichrist and his # 1 accomplice the False Prophet are captured and thrown into the lake of fire. The very same day, God confines Satan in the bottomless pit

> ***Revelation 19:19-21*** *And I saw the beast, and the kings of the earth, and their armies, gathered together to make war against him that sat on the horse, and against his army. **20** And the beast was taken, and with him the false prophet that wrought miracles before him, with which he deceived them that had received the mark of the beast, and them that worshipped his image. These both were cast alive into a lake of fire burning with brimstone. **21** And the remnant were slain with the sword of him that sat upon the horse, which sword proceeded out of his mouth: and all the fowls were filled with their flesh.*

> ***Revelation 20:1-3*** *And I saw an angel come down from heaven, having the key of the bottomless pit and a great chain in his hand. **2** And he laid hold on the dragon, that old serpent, which is the Devil, and Satan,* **and bound him a thousand years,** ***3** And cast him into the bottomless pit, and shut him up, and set a seal upon him, that he should deceive the nations no more, till the thousand years should be fulfilled: and after that he must be loosed a little season.*

END OF THE MILLENNIUM

We must leap through centuries to understand the end of Satan. Just as our present world ends with a tremendous outpouring of evil and military battles, so will the end of the Millennium. After being imprisoned for 1,000 years, God releases Satan for a brief time. Satan incites resentment and rebellion and makes one final attempt to beat God. It seems incomprehensible, after 1,000 years with Jesus Christ personally leading the world that nations rebel, and actually engage in physical war trying to dethrone King Jesus. But that is exactly what happens. Once again the main city under attack is Jerusalem. Just as Armageddon, this battle proves a losing proposition.

> *Revelation 20:7-10 And when the thousand years are expired, Satan shall be loosed out of his prison, 8 And shall go out to deceive the nations which are in the four quarters of the earth, Gog and Magog, to gather them together to battle: the number of whom is as the sand of the sea. 9 And they went up on the breadth of the earth, and compassed the camp of the saints about, and the beloved city: and fire came down from God out of heaven, and devoured them. 10 And the devil that deceived them was cast into the lake of fire and brimstone, where the beast and the false prophet are, and shall be tormented day and night for ever and ever.*

The battle ends decisively. An avalanche of fire falls from the sky devouring the enemy. Satan has led his final act of rebellion. God banishes Satan to the lake of fire. Observe the beast and the false prophet remain alive and suffering in the lake of fire. God does not use the words: death, destroy, or second death describing Satan's judgment. Revelation 20:10 describes the doctrinal, literal judgment for the satanic trinity.

Eternity's Dawn

Standing beside Jesus, his Bride (the Church) weeps. She remembers times long ago. She remembers when people fought Jesus Christ -not with guns, but with disbelief, with religion pretending to be faith, with their education and pride. But just like those boldly surrounding Jerusalem at the end of the Millennium, they fought with a determined, rebellious human heart, refusing to surrender. Audacious pride, the human stain of self-righteousness permeates the psyche of each lost soul. They want no Saviour, like Lucifer they want themselves to be like God.

Suddenly, a tremendous sound overwhelms the Bride; it rolls like thunder, growing in intensity and volume. Then great blackness engulfs everything. After a few moments, the blackness parts like a theatre's curtain revealing a Great White Throne. The one sitting upon the throne emanates light, more dreadful than a million suns. Heaven and earth flee away, hurled like a hurricane blows leaves. When the great rush passes, the galaxies are gone. Countless billions of people, stand before the throne.

A great invisible power forces all creatures to their knees. Everyone knows who sits upon the throne, the Alpha and Omega, Lord of Lords, and King of kings- the omnipotent Holy God, Jesus Christ. The Saviour men refused in life now faces them in death. The books open; God deals with each individual soul.

Angels segregate the crowds into distinct groups. Multitudes are moved and stand beside the Bride. A larger, innumerable mass of people moves toward deeper darkness. Blackness in front of them opens like a portal to another world. Suddenly, a smell wafts through the crowd, an acrid stench of sulfur and brimstone. Enormous tongues of fire, like sun spot eruptions, burst out reaching hungrily for the terrified crowds. The opening grows larger, revealing a lake of fire stretching backward into the universe.

The screaming starts, wailing and weeping from billions of souls. They try moving toward Jesus Christ, but an unseen barrier stops them. Angels begin dragging people toward the lake of fire. Wailing and gnashing teeth penetrate the vacuum of space. One by one lost souls are cast into the flames.

Finally the horror ends. The portal to the lake of fire closes and an awed and terrible silence fills time and space. With his Bride beside him, Jesus rises from his throne. Next Jesus Christ speaks a new universe into existence. Old things truly pass away and all things become new. Shimmering like a diamond, a magnificent object descends from above, heaven's crowning jewel, New Jerusalem. Jesus presents his bride with her 1,000 year anniversary present. (See Jerusalem)

New Jerusalem orbits the earth like a moon, probably hovering directly above the temple on earth. The nations below bask in her glorious light. Constant interaction between earth's Jerusalem, and New Jerusalem takes place. The Bride's status ranks high, especially in governmental responsibilities. Apparently earth's rulers, in some way, account to New Jerusalem. Observe they bring their honor and glory into the ciity. New Jerusalem is truly the jewel of heaven, perhaps even God's finest creation? The precious stones and metals emanate and reflect light and glory. Twelve pearl gates allow entrance into the city. A main street or boulevard runs through the city. The street (not streets) is made of pure gold.

CHAPTER NOTES
GREAT WHITE THRONE JUDGMENT

Revelation 20:11-15 *And I saw a great white throne, and him that sat on it, from whose face the earth and the heaven fled away; and there was found no place for them.* ***12*** *And I saw the dead, small and great, stand before God; and the books were opened: and another book was opened, which is the book of life: and the dead were judged out of those things which were written in the books, according to their works.* ***13*** *And the sea gave up the dead which were in it; and death and hell delivered up the dead which were in them: and they were judged every man according to their works.* ***14*** *And death and hell were cast into the lake of fire. This is the second death.* ***15*** *And whosoever was not found written in the book of life was cast into the lake of fire.*

Philippians 2:10-11 *That at the name of Jesus every knee should bow, of things in heaven, and things in earth, and things under the earth;* ***11*** *And that every tongue should confess that Jesus Christ is Lord, to the glory of God the Father.*

Revelation 20:15 *And whosoever was not found written in the book of life was cast into the lake of fire.*

Matthew 13:40-42 *As therefore the tares are gathered and burned in the fire; so shall it be in the end of this world.* ***41*** *The Son of man shall send forth his angels, and they shall gather out of his kingdom all things that offend, and them which do iniquity;* ***42*** *And shall cast them into a furnace of fire: there shall be wailing and gnashing of teeth.*

Matthew 13:47-50 *Again, the kingdom of heaven is like unto a net, that was cast into the sea, and gathered of every kind:* ***48*** *Which, when it was full, they drew to shore, and sat down, and gathered the good into vessels, but cast the bad away.* ***49*** *So shall* *it be at the end of the world: the angels shall come forth, and sever the wicked from among the just, 50 And shall cast them into the furnace of fire: there shall be wailing and gnashing of teeth.*

Matthew 25:41 *Then shall he say also unto them on the left hand, Depart from me, ye cursed, into everlasting fire, prepared for the devil and his angels::*

New heaven. New earth. New Jerusalem.

Isaiah 51:6 *Lift up your eyes to the heavens, and look upon the earth beneath: for the heavens shall vanish away like smoke, and the earth shall wax old like a garment, and they that dwell therein shall die in like manner: but my salvation shall be for ever, and my righteousness shall not be abolished.*

2 Peter 3:12-13 *Looking for and hasting unto the coming of the day of God, wherein the heavens being on fire shall be dissolved, and the elements shall melt with fervent heat? 13 Nevertheless we, according to his promise, look for new heavens and a new earth, wherein dwelleth righteousness.*

New Jerusalem

Revelation 21:1-2 *And I saw a new heaven and a new earth: for the first heaven and the first earth were passed away; and there was no more sea. 2 And I John saw the holy city, new Jerusalem, coming down from God out of heaven, prepared as a bride adorned for her husband.*

Revelation 21:9-11 *And there came unto me one of the seven angels which had the seven vials full of the seven last plagues, and* *talked with me, saying, Come hither, I will shew thee the bride, the Lamb's wife.* **10** *And he carried me away in the spirit to a great and high mountain, and shewed me that great city, the holy Jerusalem, descending out of heaven from God,* **11** *Having the glory of God: and her light was like unto a stone most precious, even like a jasper stone, clear as crystal;;*

Revelation 21:16 *And the city lieth foursquare, and the length is as large as the breadth: and he measured the city with the reed, twelve thousand furlongs. The length and the breadth and the height of it are equal.*

(The "sea" mentioned in verse *Re. 21:1* is a reference to the deep in *Gen. 1:2-3*. With the deep gone, things are as they were *in the beginning*; No longer are there any barriers restricting God's creation.)

Revelation 21:23-27 *And the city had no need of the sun, neither of the moon, to shine in it: for the glory of God did lighten it, and the Lamb is the light thereof.* **24** *And the nations of them which are saved shall walk in the light of it: and the kings of the earth do bring their glory and honour into it.* **25** *And the gates of it shall not be shut at all by day: for there shall be no night there.* **26** *And they shall bring the glory and honour of the nations into it.* **27** *And there shall in no wise enter into it any thing that defileth, neither whatsoever worketh abomination, or maketh a lie: but they which are written in the Lamb's book of life.*

Revelation 21:12-20 *And had a wall great and high, and had twelve gates, and at the gates twelve angels, and names written thereon, which are the names of the twelve tribes of the children of Israel:* **13** *On the east three gates; on the north three gates; on the south three gates; and on the west three gates.* **14** *And the wall of the city had twelve foundations, and in them the names of the twelve* *apostles of the Lamb. 15 And he that talked with me had a golden reed to measure the city, and the gates thereof, and the wall thereof. 16 And the city lieth foursquare, and the length is as large as the breadth: and he measured the city with the reed, twelve thousand furlongs. The length and the breadth and the height of it are equal. 17 And he measured the wall thereof, an hundred and forty and four cubits, according to the measure of a man, that is, of the angel. 18 And the building of the wall of it was of jasper: and the city was pure gold, like unto clear glass. 19 And the foundations of the wall of the city were garnished with all manner of precious stones. The first foundation was jasper; the second, sapphire; the third, a chalcedony; the fourth, an emerald; 20 The fifth, sardonyx; the sixth, sardius; the seventh, chrysolite; the eighth, beryl; the ninth, a topaz; the tenth, a chrysoprasus; the eleventh, a jacinth; the twelfth, an amethyst.*

Revelation 21:21 *And the twelve gates were twelve pearls; every several gate was of one pearl: and the street of the city was pure gold, as it were transparent glass.*

Those Who Remain

So Christians have their new home in New Jerusalem, but what about people not part of the Church? What about saved people from the Millennium, the Tribulation, Old Testament saints, persons who died under an age of accountability?

Think about what these people just went through. First a great resurrection brought billions of people to the Great White Throne. Then heaven and earth dissolved with fire. Then final judgment takes place and the lake of fire swallows most the crowd. God creates a new heaven and a new earth. And now they wait together on the new earth for whatever happens next. Eternal Zion, the city on the sides of the North- remains on the new earth as it houses the Throne and the Temple of God.

God's original plan begins again. God has not repented from his original intention; thus populating the earth commences:

Romans 11:29, For the gifts and calling of God are without repentance.

Genesis 1:28 And God blessed them, and God said unto them, Be fruitful, and multiply, and replenish the earth, and subdue it: and have dominion over the fish of the sea, and over the fowl of the air, and over every living thing that moveth upon the earth.

GOD SAID ALMOST THE SAME THINGS TO NOAH AFTER THE FLOOD.

>*Genesis 9:1-2 And God blessed Noah and his sons, and said unto them, Be fruitful, and multiply, and replenish the earth. 2 And the fear of you and the dread of you shall be upon every beast of the earth, and upon every fowl of the air, upon all that moveth upon the earth, and upon all the fishes of the sea; into your hand are they delivered.*

The children of the kingdom reach an age of maturity, and eat from the tree of life. The fruit transforms mortal bodies giving them immortality. After the earth reaches full capacity, populating the universe begins and continues forever.

>*Isaiah 9:7 Of the increase of his government and peace there shall be no end, upon the throne of David, and upon his kingdom, to order it, and to establish it with judgment and with justice from henceforth even for ever. The zeal of the LORD of hosts will perform this*

>*Revelation 2:7 He that hath an ear, let him hear what the Spirit saith unto the churches; To him that overcometh will I give to eat of the tree of life, which is in the midst of the paradise of God.*

>*Revelation 22:2 In the midst of the street of it, and on either side of the river, was there the tree of life, which bare twelve manner of fruits, and yielded her fruit every month: and the leaves of the tree were for the healing of the nations.*

Defining the Church

§

IDENTIFYING CHRISTIANITY IN A DOCTRINAL and historical sense is imperative, because it defines who is not a Christian. Abraham, Isaac, Rebecca, Moses, and King David -all saved believers, and live forever in heaven, but they are not Christians. The biblical names of the church are: The Church, The Body of Christ, The Bride, Chaste Virgin, and Lamb's Wife. Christianity did not exist until New Testament times. Unique and exclusive truths exist for different groups of people in God's Kingdom. Things different are not the same. One must rightly divide the Bible to understand the kingdom.

2 Timothy 2:15 Study to shew thyself approved unto God, a workman that needeth not to be ashamed, rightly dividing the word of truth.

Ephesians 1:22-23 And hath put all things under his feet, and gave him to be the head over all things to the church, Which is his body, the fulness of him that filleth all in all.

Ephesians 5:30 For we are members of his body, of his flesh, and of his bones.

Acts 11:26 And when he had found him, he brought him unto Antioch. And it came to pass, that a whole year they assembled themselves with the church, and taught much people. And the disciples were called Christians first in Antioch.

John 3:29 He that hath the bride is the bridegroom: but the friend of the bridegroom, which standeth and heareth him, rejoiceth greatly because of the bridegroom's voice: this my joy therefore is fulfilled.

2 Corinthians 11:2-3 For I am jealous over you with godly jealousy: for I have espoused you to one husband, that I may present you as a chaste virgin to Christ. 3 But I fear, lest by any means, as the serpent beguiled Eve through his subtilty, so your minds should be corrupted from the simplicity that is in Christ.

Revelation 21:2 2 And I John saw the holy city, new Jerusalem, coming down from God out of heaven, prepared as a bride adorned for her husband.

Revelation 21:9 And there came unto me one of the seven angels which had the seven vials full of the seven last plagues, and talked with me, saying, Come hither, I will shew thee the bride, the Lamb's wife.

1 Corinthians 12:12-14 For as the body is one, and hath many members, and all the members of that one body, being many, are one body: so also is Christ. 13 For by one Spirit are we all baptized into one body, whether we be Jews or Gentiles, whether we be bond or free; and have been all made to drink into one Spirit. 14 For **the body** is not one member, but many.

Acts 20:28 Take heed therefore unto yourselves, and to all the flock, over the which the Holy Ghost hath made you overseers, to feed the church of God, which he hath purchased with his own blood.

Dying

AFTER DEATH CHRISTIANS' SOULS GOING to the 3rd heaven. As we learned from our study of the universe, this is a very long way from planet earth, literally billions of light years. For sake of clear understanding, it helps immensely if one thinks of the third heaven as a distant place rather than a mystical dimension. The map of the cosmos remains essential for understanding heaven as the place Christians go after death.

When a Christians die their souls go to the 3rd heaven immediately. There is not an intermediate period of soul sleep. Exactly what happens to a Christian's soul must, however, be proved with scripture. Since many persons believe in the doctrine of soul sleep, it is expedient to consider this other point of view.

WHAT IS SOUL SLEEP?

Soul sleep is the belief when Christians die they enter a state of unconsciousness as if they were sleeping, sort of suspended animation. In other words a Christian loses consciousness in death, and the next thing experienced would be the Rapture.

WHY DO SOME CHRISTIANS BELIEVE IN SOUL SLEEP?

There are several passages of scripture calling a Christian's death sleep. In fact the word sleep is a synonym for the Christian's death.

If soul sleep is incorrect, then it becomes necessary for precise and accurate reasons from scripture to refute the idea. To simply say I do not believe in a doctrine without knowing why is unsatisfactory. Christians should know how to defend what they believe with proof texts from the Bible. Below passages from the Bible constituting reasons some Christians believe in soul sleep. Clearly God is equating death (at least physical death) with sleep.

> *1 Thessalonians 4:13-18 13 But I would not have you to be ignorant, brethren, concerning them which are asleep, that ye sorrow not, even as others which have no hope. 14 For if we believe that Jesus died and rose again, even so them also which sleep in Jesus will God bring with him. 15 For this we say unto you by the word of the Lord, that we which are alive and remain unto the coming of the Lord shall not prevent them which are asleep.*

> *1 Corinthians 11:30 For this cause many are weak and sickly among you, and many sleep.*

> *1 Corinthians 15:51 Behold, I shew you a mystery; We shall not all sleep, but we shall all be changed,*

> *Acts 7:59-60 And they stoned Stephen, calling upon God, and saying, Lord Jesus, receive my spirit. 60 And he kneeled down, and cried with a loud voice, Lord, lay not this sin to their charge. And when he had said this, he fell asleep.*

As we can see from the above verses, it is not foolishness to believe the doctrine of soul sleep. If these verses were the only passages dealing with a believer's death then soul sleep would certainly be possible, but these texts are not the only verses. God gives us many other verses dealing with death.

God used the word *sleep* describing death because death appears to the living like someone sleeping. In other words, when a person loses a loved one, the living can best understand their loss by thinking of them as being asleep. As we continue our study, it is important to weigh all the verses dealing with life after death.

Christians do not get their immortal physical bodies as soon as they die. All Christians receive their new immortal bodies at the same time, at an appointed day in the future. This day is commonly referred to as the Rapture. Whether Christians died recently or within the last 2,000 years, all Christians receive new bodies at the same time.

When the Bible teaches us about our bodies in heaven, God often contrasts the state of our bodies while on earth. Read the verses below and consider the juxtaposition.

> ***Corinthians 15: 52*** *In a moment, in the twinkling of an eye, at the last trump: for the trumpet shall sound, and the dead shall be raised incorruptible, and we shall be changed. 53 For this corruptible must put on incorruption, and this mortal must put on immortality*

Synonyms describing a Christian's body while alive on earth **before going to heaven**: Earthly house, tabernacle, flesh, corruptible, dead body, mortal, bondage of corruption.

Synonyms used to describe a Christian's body **after going to heaven**: Building of God, house not made with hands, incorruptible, house from heaven, immortal.

> ***Romans 8:10-11*** *And if Christ be in you, the body is dead because of sin; but the Spirit is life because of righteousness. 11 But if the Spirit of him that raised up Jesus from the dead dwell in you, he that raised up Christ from the dead shall also quicken your mortal bodies by his Spirit that dwelleth in you.*

> **Romans 8:21-23** *Because the creature itself also shall be delivered from the bondage of corruption into the glorious liberty of the children of God. 22 For we know that the whole creation groaneth travaileth in pain together until now. 23 And not only they, but ourselves also, which have the firstfruits of the Spirit, even we ourselves groan within ourselves, waiting for the adoption, to wit, the redemption of our body.*

Since Christians do not get their new physical bodies until the Rapture, what does this mean for Christians who die before the Rapture? Can a soul live without a physical body?

> **2 Corinthians 5:1-9** *For we know that if our earthly house of this tabernacle were dissolved, we have a building of God, an house not made with hands, eternal in the heavens. 2 For in this we groan, earnestly desiring to be clothed upon with our house which is from heaven: 3 If so be that being clothed we shall not be found naked. 4 For we that are in this tabernacle do groan, being burdened: not for that we would be unclothed, but clothed upon, that mortality might be swallowed up of life. 5 Now he that hath wrought us for the selfsame thing is God, who also hath given unto us the earnest of the Spirit. 6 Therefore we are always confident, knowing that, whilst we are at home in the body, we are absent from the Lord: 7 (For we walk by faith, not by sight:) 8 We are confident, I say, and willing rather to be absent from the body, and to be present with the Lord. 9 Wherefore we labour, that, whether present or absent, we may be accepted of him.*

THOUGHT TO PONDER:

As we examine the evidence happening to a Christian after death, a possible interpretation from *2 Cor.5:1* A Christian's soul may have a temporary physical body before it receives a permanent vessel at the Rapture. It is also possible a Christian receives no physical body until the Rapture. If this is the case then the verse is simply indicating the body is promised in the future. A soul does not require a physical body to exist.

Paul is willing to be absent from the body and present with the Lord. A Christian is present with the Lord immediately after physical death. A soul has a spiritual body independent of its physical dwelling. Most importantly it seems a state of awareness or consciousness is established immediately. The soul possesses an intelligent, conscious existence outside a physical body. This fact is shown clearly in the passage below:

> *2 Corinthians 12:2-4 I knew a man in Christ above fourteen years ago, (whether in the body, I cannot tell; or whether out of the body, I cannot tell: God knoweth;) such an one caught up to the third heaven. 3 And I knew such a man, (whether in the body, or out of the body, I cannot tell: God knoweth;) 4 How that he was caught up into paradise, and heard unspeakable words, which it is not lawful for a man to utter.*

Is there more evidence proving we go to heaven immediately and conscious state after death? Yes. The Apostle Paul adds more insight. Notice he says dying is gain, and if he departs (dies) he will be with Christ immediately.

> *Philippians 1:20-24 According to my earnest expectation and my hope, that in nothing I shall be ashamed, but that with all boldness, as always, so now also Christ shall be magnified in my body, whether it be by life, or by death. 21 For to me to live is Christ, and to die is gain. 22 But if I live in the flesh, this is the fruit of my labour: yet what I shall choose I wot not. 23 For I am in a strait betwixt two, having a desire to depart, and to be with Christ; which is far better: 24 Nevertheless to abide in the flesh is more needful for you. Jesus also deals with the question of saved*

people being conscious and in heaven as soon as they die. Consider the following discourse Jesus is having with the Sadducees about the resurrection.

Mark 12:26-27 *And as touching the dead, that they rise: have ye not read in the book of Moses, how in the bush God spake unto him, saying, I am the God of Abraham, and the God of Isaac, and the God of Jacob? 27 He is not the God of the dead, but the God of the living: ye therefore do greatly err.*

The salient point of Jesus' answer is Abraham, Isaac, and Jacob were alive when God made the statement to Moses from the burning bush. Therefore, we conclude God's people do not simply go into some sort of suspended animation (soul sleep) when they die. In a very direct way, Jesus' answer is the clearest statement refuting soul.

Christian Living after Death

THIS STUDY MARCHES CHRISTIANS THROUGH the first 1000 years of heaven immediately following the Rapture. We take this walk quickly, and then go back over it filling in details.

In chronological order beginning with the Rapture

1. The Rapture (immortal body received)
2. Judgment Seat of Christ
3. The Marriage
4. 2nd Coming (Christians return to earth with Jesus)
5. Armageddon
6. Millennium
7. Great White Throne Judgment
8. New Jerusalem (Christians' home for eternity
9. Eternity

Rapture

THE CHURCH, ALSO CALLED THE Bride of Christ and the Body of Christ is entirely formed of believers in Jesus Christ. Church members are called Christians. All members are saved (born again) citizens in the kingdom of God. Christians include Jews and Gentiles. Although some theological debate as to the exact moment the Church began, all agree it started in New Testament times. The church age end priors to Jesus' 2nd Advent; therefore, the number of Christians is finite. For the last 2,000 years God has added souls to his Church, but soon he calls the last generation of living Christians to heaven, an event commonly referred to as the Rapture. Once the Body of Jesus Christ is complete, Jesus removes it off the earth. Although the Church includes saved Jews, it is overwhelmingly Gentile; therefore, Jesus refers to the completion of His Bride as the *fullness of the Gentiles.*

> **Romans 11:25** *For I would not, brethren, that ye should be ignorant of this mystery, lest ye should be wise in your own conceits; that blindness in part is happened to Israel, until the fulness of the Gentiles be come in.*

When the Bride is complete, Jesus gathers all Christians who ever lived to one location in the 3rd heaven. The final generation Christians never die physically, they receive immortal bodies and are taken to heaven in an instant. This tremendous supernatural event is the Rapture.

Immediately after the Rapture, people still live on earth. Life goes on for regular human beings. And while God does business with Christians in the 3rd heaven, the great tribulation takes place on earth.

SCRIPTURAL EVIDENCE FOR THE RAPTURE

1 Corinthians 15:50-58 Now this I say, brethren, that flesh and blood cannot inherit the kingdom of God; neither doth corruption inherit incorruption. 51 Behold, I shew you a mystery; We shall not all sleep, but we shall all be changed, 52 In a moment, in the twinkling of an eye, at the last trump: for the trumpet shall sound, and the dead shall be raised incorruptible, and we shall be changed. 53 For this corruptible must put on incorruption, and this mortal must put on immortality. 54 So when this corruptible shall have put on incorruption, and this mortal shall have put on immortality, then shall be brought to pass the saying that is written, Death is swallowed up in victory. 55 O death, where is thy sting? O grave, where is thy victory? 56 The sting of death is sin; and the strength of sin is the law. 57 But thanks be to God, which giveth us the victory through our Lord Jesus Christ. 58 Therefore, my beloved brethren, be ye stedfast, unmoveable, always abounding in the work of the Lord, forasmuch as ye know that your labour is not in vain in the Lord..

1 Thessalonians 4:13-18 But I would not have you to be ignorant, brethren, concerning them which are asleep, that ye sorrow not, even as others which have no hope. 14 For if we believe that Jesus died and rose again, even so them also which sleep in Jesus will God bring with him. 15 For this we say unto you by the word of the Lord, that we which are alive and remain unto the coming of the Lord shall not prevent them which are asleep. **16** *For the Lord himself shall descend from heaven with a shout, with the voice of the archangel, and with the trump of God: and the dead in Christ shall rise first:* **17** *Then we which are alive and remain shall be caught up together with them in the clouds, to meet the Lord in the air: and so shall we ever be with the Lord.* **18** *Wherefore comfort one another with these words.*

Judgment Seat of Christ

§

Step Two

ALTHOUGH CHRISTIANS ENJOY ETERNAL SECURITY, we still face a coming judgment. The Christian's judgment takes place at the Judgment Seat of Christ (JSC). Even though everyone at the JSC goes to heaven; God requires an accounting for the way each Christian behaved. Make no mistake-be ye warned; a Christian is responsible for the way he/she lives. The JSC deals with unrepented sins on an individual basis. To be perfectly candid, judge yourself and repent here and now, or have Jesus Christ deal with you at the JSC. God defines a Christian's sins as works of the flesh, and works determines personal rewards and inheritance.

> *Romans 14:10-12 But why dost thou judge thy brother? or why dost thou set at nought thy brother? for we shall all stand before the judgment seat of Christ. 11 For it is written, As I live, saith the Lord, every knee shall bow to me, and every tongue shall confess to God. 12 So then every one of us shall give account of himself to God.*

> *2 Corinthians 5:8-11 We are confident, I say, and willing rather to be absent from the body, and to be present with the Lord. 9 Wherefore we labour, that, whether present or absent, we may be accepted of him.* **10 For we must all appear before the judgment seat of Christ; that every one may receive the things done in his body, according to that he hath done, whether it**

be good or bad. 11 Knowing therefore the terror of the Lord, we persuade men; but we are made manifest unto God; and I trust also are made manifest in your consciences.

Notice this judgment concerns labor, which is works. After salvation, a Christian's good works earns rewards. Likewise bad works result in lost rewards. Thus, a portion of a Christian's inheritance can be earned or lost. Observe God uses the word terror to describe the judgment. No one goes to hell from the Judgment Seat of Christ, but no doubt, it will be a tough day.

Colossians 3:23-25 And whatsoever ye do, do it heartily, as to the Lord, and not unto men; 24 Knowing that of the Lord ye shall receive the reward of the inheritance: for ye serve the Lord Christ. 25 But he that doeth wrong shall receive for the wrong which he hath done: and there is no respect of persons.

In the passage below Paul likens a Christian's good works to gold, silver, precious stones; while bad works are likened to wood, hay, and stubble. These works add to salvation's sure foundation. *In 1Cor. 3:15*, observe even if a Christian's works burn up, he is still saved. The verse proves eternal security. Just imagine a Christian's works burning up, and the Christian is left standing there with nothing to show for his life on earth. Mercifully, he is still saved based on the finished work of Jesus Christ. Works have nothing to do with earning salvation- but they do earn an inheritance and eternal rewards.

1 Corinthians 3:11-15 For other foundation can no man lay than that is laid, which is Jesus Christ. 12 Now if any man build upon this foundation gold, silver, precious stones, wood, hay, stubble; 13 Every man's work shall be made manifest: for the day shall declare it, because it shall be revealed by fire; and the fire shall try every man's work of what sort it is. 14 If any man's work abide which he hath built thereupon, he shall receive a reward. **15 If any man's work shall be burned, he shall suffer loss: but he himself shall be saved; yet so as by fire.**

Judgment Seat of Christ (JSC) Thinking
about works

Christians often become confused defining a difference between works and sins. Wisdom commends us to let the Bible define bad works, or works of the flesh. Consider this passage from Galatians 5.

> *Galatians 5:16-21 This I say then, Walk in the Spirit, and ye shall not fulfil the lust of the flesh. 17 For the flesh lusteth against the Spirit, and the Spirit against the flesh: and these are contrary the one to the other: so that ye cannot do the things that ye would. 18 But if ye be led of the Spirit, ye are not under the law. 19 Now the works of the flesh are manifest, which are these; Adultery, fornication, uncleanness, lasciviousness, 20 Idolatry, witchcraft, hatred, variance, emulations, wrath, strife, seditions, heresies, 21 Envyings, murders, drunkenness, revellings, and such like: of the which I tell you before, as I have also told you in time past, that they which do such things shall not inherit the kingdom of God.*

Scripture clearly defines *works of the flesh* as sins. Again God warns about having no inheritance in the Kingdom of God. A Christian receives an earnest payment of inheritance upon salvation when they receive the Holy Ghost; therefore, part of a Christian's inheritance cannot be lost. The man whose works went up in smoke exemplifies Christians who lose everything they should have earned. Salvation, itself, has nothing to do with works.

> *Ephesians 1:13-14 In whom ye also trusted, after that ye heard the word of truth, the gospel of your salvation: in whom also after that ye believed, ye were sealed with that holy Spirit of promise, 14*

Which is the earnest of our inheritance until the redemption of the purchased possession, unto the praise of his glory.

2 Corinthians 5:11 *Knowing therefore the terror of the Lord, we persuade men; but we are made manifest unto God; and I trust also are made manifest in your consciences.*

As previously mentioned, *knowing the terror of the Lord*, declares a warning to saved people! Once the full gravity of the JSC is grasped an emotion akin to panic ensues. No doubt all Christians have some areas in their lives that need attention. Thus the urgent question is asked,

Is there anything I can do now for my bad works so I won't have to face them at the Judgment Seat of Christ?

Mercifully, the answer is yes. No Christian lives a perfect sinless life. And God is not going to bring up every mistake you ever made at the Judgment Seat of Christ. God makes provision for our failures. When we sin, we should confess to God and repent. If we do this God pardons our bad works. Only unrepented bad works are dealt with at the JSC.

1 John 1:9 *If we confess our sins, he is faithful and just to forgive us our sins, and to cleanse us from all unrighteousness.*

1ˢᵗ John 1:9 is one of the greatest promises in the Bible to the Christian. It is not a salvation verse; confessing sins does not save anyone. This is a Christian getting right verse. But even with this great a promise, let us not kid ourselves. Repentance is required to delete our bad works from God's memory. Beware, often Christians ask God to forgive them for their sins, but what they're really asking is for God to excuse them for their sin.

Proverbs 28:13 He that covereth his sins shall not prosper: but whoso confesseth and forsaketh them shall have mercy.

Psalms 103:8-12 The LORD is merciful and gracious, slow to anger, and plenteous in mercy. 9 He will not always chide: neither will he keep his anger for ever. 10 He hath not dealt with us after our sins; nor rewarded us according to our iniquities. 11 For as the heaven is high above the earth, so great is his mercy toward them that fear him. 12 As far as the east is from the west, so far hath he removed our transgressions from us.

Another extension of God's mercy (and warning) extends every time Christians take the Lord's Supper. The purpose of the supper is to remember Jesus' sacrificial death, and for Christians to solemnly consider the way they live. If bad works need confessed and repented---JUST DO IT! If you judge yourself and repent you can settle the problem here and now. Bad behavior truly forsaken will not be brought up at the JSC.

1 Corinthians 11:28-31 But let a man examine himself, and so let him eat of that bread, and drink of that cup. 29 For he that eateth and drinketh unworthily, eateth and drinketh damnation to himself, not discerning the Lord's body. 30 For this cause many are weak and sickly among you, and many sleep. 31 For if we would judge ourselves, we should not be judged.

CROWNS EARNED OR LOST

Good works inherit eternal rewards. The Bible mentions five crowns a Christian may earn. What eternal rewards these crowns bring is not fully disclosed. No doubt the reward is abundantly more than we can imagine. I believe the crowns represent more than pieces of medal given back to Jesus. The crowns represent eternal possessions for what a Christian's earns.

CROWN OF LIFE, the martyr's crown, special reward given to those who suffer great persecution and even death for Jesus' sake.

> ***Revelation 2:10*** *Fear none of those things which thou shalt suffer: behold, the devil shall cast some of you into prison, that ye may be tried; and ye shall have tribulation ten days: be thou faithful unto death, and I will give thee a crown of life.*

> ***James 1:12*** *Blessed is the man that endureth temptation: for when he is tried, he shall receive the crown of life, which the Lord hath promised to them that love him.*

CROWN OF GLORY, the elder or pastor's crown. All who teach or disciple other Christians may earn this crown. This crown available to anyone who helps instruct the body of Christ. This includes teaching your own children. Beware- those who teach for sake of money or pride exempt themselves from this reward. Consequently, just because one pastors or teaches does not guarantee the crown of glory; it must be earned.

> ***1 Peter 5:2-4*** *Feed the flock of God which is among you, taking the oversight thereof, not by constraint, but willingly; not for filthy lucre, but of a ready mind; 3 Neither as being lords over God's heritage, but being ensamples to the flock. 4 And when the chief Shepherd shall appear, ye shall receive a crown of glory that fadeth not away.*

CROWN OF REJOICING, the soul winner's crown. A crown for Christians who lead lost people to Jesus Christ. How sad it is so many Christians do not even try to win the lost. Pass out tracts, tell people about Jesus- God will reward your efforts here on earth and then again at the judgment seat of Christ.

1 Thessalonians 2:19-20 For what is our hope, or joy, or crown of rejoicing? Are not even ye in the presence of our Lord Jesus Christ at his coming? 20 For ye are our glory and joy.

Philippians 4:1 Therefore, my brethren dearly beloved and longed for, my joy and crown, so stand fast in the Lord, my dearly beloved.

CROWN OF RIGHTEOUSNESS, for those who love the Lord's, those living as if the Lord returns at any moment, Christians steadfastly keeping the faith.

2 Timothy 4:5-8 But watch thou in all things, endure afflictions, do the work of an evangelist, make full proof of thy ministry. 6 For I am now ready to be offered, and the time of my departure is at hand. 7 I have fought a good fight, I have finished my course, I have kept the faith: 8 Henceforth there is laid up for me a crown of righteousness, which the Lord, the righteous judge, shall give me at that day: and not to me only, but unto all them also that love his appearing.

INCORRUPTIBLE CROWN, The crown of victory. For those who keep their bodies under subjection, a reward for those resisting the lusts of the flesh. A good witness and solid testimony.

1 Corinthians 9:25-27 And every man that striveth for the mastery is temperate in all things. Now they do it to obtain a corruptible crown; but we an incorruptible. 26 I therefore so run, not as uncertainly; so fight I, not as one that beateth the air: 27 But I keep under my body, and bring it into subjection: lest that by any means, when I have preached to others, I myself should be a castaway.

Marriage of the Lamb

§

STEP THREE

THE BIBLE SAYS THE BRIDE makes herself ready just prior to the 2nd coming of Jesus Christ. Presently the church is only engaged to Jesus Christ. Just like a human bride makes herself completely ready just before her wedding day- so must the Bride of Jesus Christ prepare before her marriage. Although salvation promises Christians heaven, a few things still need ironed out. The Judgment Seat of Christ fully prepares the Bride (Christians) for the wedding.

> *Revelation 19:7-9 Let us be glad and rejoice, and give honour to him: for the marriage of the Lamb is come, and his wife hath made herself ready. 8 And to her was granted that she should be arrayed in fine linen, clean and white: for the fine linen is the righteousness of saints. 9 And he saith unto me, Write, Blessed are they which are called unto the marriage supper of the Lamb. And he saith unto me, These are the true sayings of God.*

Notice the Bride is now being called the Lamb's Wife. The Marriage of the Lamb takes place in *Revelation 19* and the Second Coming takes place in Revelation 20. While the Judgment Seat of Christ and the Marriage of the Lamb take place in the 3rd heaven, the Tribulation is happening on earth.

The Marriage takes place in the 3rd heaven in a Palace. Notice those called guests at the marriage supper of the Lamb. Wedding guests attend the Bride's marriage. Do not confuse the guests with the Bride. Christians are the Bride; they are not the guests. Things different are not the same.

Who are these persons invited to the Marriage Supper? Prophetically, they represent the Jewish virgins discussed in *Matthew 25* See also Psalm 45. The Marriage of the Lamb is a big social event in heaven. Practically, (admittedly a bit of speculating) the wedding invitation list may well include people like: Moses, David, Ruth, John the Baptist, Tribulation saints, etc. Sadly, many Israelites invited refuse to come. (See author's work *What Might the Parable Be?)*

> *Matthew 22:2-4 2 The kingdom of heaven is like unto a certain king, which made a marriage for his son, 3 And sent forth his servants to call them that were bidden to the wedding: and they would not come.*

> *Matthew 25:1-2 1 Then shall the kingdom of heaven be likened unto ten virgins, which took their lamps, and went forth to meet the bridegroom. 2 And five of them were wise, and five were foolish.*

A window into the Marriage Supper is found in Psalm 45. Observe the event happens in heaven, because it is for God. God the Father addresses God the Son as King *Ps.45:6, 7* The first 8 verses discuss Jesus Christ; he is honored in a public ceremony. The event is not for any human king on earth because his throne is forever. And he is called God.

The Lord *the King* desires the beauty of his *Queen* who shows up in *45:9.* Notice she stands at the King's right hand. The Bride becomes the Queen because the marriage takes place. This event is the Marriage Supper or the reception. *45:9-17,* the narrative discusses the Queen. The Queen is told to worship the King (who is called God by God). The Queen's companions are virgins; this coincides perfectly with the five virgins who were ready to meet the Bridegroom (see Matthew 25, parable of the ten virgins). The Psalm commemorates forever Jesus' wedding, and the people on the earth praise his Bride.

Psalms 45:1-17 To the chief Musician upon Shoshannim, for the sons of Korah, Maschil, A Song of loves. My heart is inditing a good matter: I speak of the things which I have made touching the king: my tongue is the pen of a ready writer. **2** *Thou art fairer than the children of men: grace is poured into thy lips: therefore God hath blessed thee for ever.* **3** *Gird thy sword upon thy thigh, O most mighty, with thy glory and thy majesty.* **4** *And in thy majesty ride prosperously because of truth and meekness and righteousness; and thy right hand shall teach thee terrible things.* **5** *Thine arrows are sharp in the heart of the king's enemies; whereby the people fall under thee.* **6** *Thy throne, O God, is for ever and ever: the sceptre of thy kingdom is a right sceptre.* **7** *Thou lovest righteousness, and hatest wickedness: therefore God, thy God, hath anointed thee with the oil of gladness above thy fellows.* **8** *All thy garments smell of myrrh, and aloes, and cassia, out of the ivory palaces, whereby they have made thee glad.* **9** *Kings' daughters were among thy honourable women: upon thy right hand did stand the queen in gold of Ophir.* **10** *Hearken, O daughter, and consider, and incline thine ear; forget also thine own people, and thy father's house;* **11** *So shall the king greatly desire thy beauty: for he is thy Lord; and worship thou him.* **12** *And the daughter of Tyre shall be there with a gift; even the rich among the people shall intreat thy favour.* **13** *The king's daughter is all glorious within: her clothing is of wrought gold.* **14** *She shall be brought unto the king in raiment of needlework: the virgins her companions that follow her shall be brought unto thee.* **15** *With gladness and rejoicing shall they be brought: they shall enter into the king's palace.* **16** *Instead of thy fathers shall be thy children, whom thou mayest make princes in all the earth.* **17** *I will make thy name to be remembered in all generations: therefore shall the people praise thee for ever and ever..*

The Second Coming

STEP FOUR

CHRISTIANS RETURN WITH JESUS AT his second coming. And it seems everyone rides their own horse. This proves animals exist in heaven. Thus after getting judged and getting married in the 3rd heaven, we travel back to earth. And by the way, Christians seem to be in the cavalry division of God's army.

> *Revelation 19:19 And I saw the beast, and the kings of the earth, and their armies, gathered together to make war against him that sat on the horse, and against his army.*

> *Revelation 19:14-15 And the armies which were in heaven followed him upon white horses, clothed in fine linen, white and clean. 15 And out of his mouth goeth a sharp sword, that with it he should smite the nations: and he shall rule them with a rod of iron: and he treadeth the winepress of the fierceness and wrath of Almighty God.*

To prove *the armies which were in heaven* include the Bride of Christ: Observe the army wears clean and white linen. The same clothing the Lamb's wife wore for the marriage in *Re. 19:7-8.*

> *Revelation 19:7-8 Let us be glad and rejoice, and give honour to him: for the marriage of the Lamb is come, and his wife hath made*

herself ready. 8 And to her was granted that she should be arrayed in fine linen, clean and white: for the fine linen is the righteousness of saints.

Scripture calls Christians soldiers twice. *Thessalonians 3:13* references the 2nd Coming. Notice Jesus comes with his saints. Since the Church is in the 3rd heaven with Jesus, the Church returns with Jesus.

2 Timothy 2:3-4 Thou therefore endure hardness, as a good soldier of Jesus Christ. 4 No man that warreth entangleth himself with the affairs of this life; that he may please him who hath chosen him to be a soldier.

1 Thessalonians 3:13 To the end he may stablish your hearts unblameable in holiness before God, even our Father, at the coming of our Lord Jesus Christ with all his saints.

War, Armageddon

§

Step Five

The Tribulation's last day is a battle named Armageddon. The very first day back on earth Christians engage in the greatest battle ever fought in human history. As Jesus Christ returns to earth, the world's armies, under guidance of Antichrist, gather in the valley of Megiddo. They aspire to destroy Jesus Christ. Honeymoons, always quite memorable, but nothing gets a marriage going like Armageddon.

So here is a sobering dose of reality. Upon returning to earth, Christians find themselves in the largest, most bloody war ever fought on planet earth (in the last 6,000 years). The battle appears short, perhaps lasting only minutes?

Revelation 16:14-16 For they are the spirits of devils, working miracles, which go forth unto the kings of the earth and of the whole world, to gather them to the battle of that great day of God Almighty. 15 Behold, I come as a thief. Blessed is he that watcheth, and keepeth his garments, lest he walk naked, and they see his shame. 16 And he gathered them together into a place called in the Hebrew tongue Armageddon.

Revelation 19:11-21 And I saw heaven opened, and behold a white horse; and he that sat upon him was called Faithful and True, and in righteousness he doth judge and make war. **12** *His eyes were as a flame of fire, and on his head were many crowns; and he had a name written, that no man knew, but he himself.* **13** *And he was clothed with a vesture dipped in blood: and his name is called The Word of God.* **14** *And the armies which were in heaven followed him upon white horses, clothed in fine linen, white and clean.* **15** *And out of his mouth goeth a sharp sword, that with it he should smite the nations: and he shall rule them with a rod of iron: and he treadeth the winepress of the fierceness and wrath of Almighty God.* **16** *And he hath on his vesture and on his thigh a name writ-ten,* KING OF KINGS, AND LORD OF LORDS. **17** *And I saw an angel standing in the sun; and he cried with a loud voice, saying to all the fowls that fly in the midst of heaven, Come and gather yourselves together unto the supper of the great God;* **18** *That ye may eat the flesh of kings, and the flesh of captains, and the flesh of mighty men, and the flesh of horses, and of them that sit on them, and the flesh of all men, both free and bond, both small and great.* **19** *And I saw the beast, and the kings of the earth, and their armies, gathered together to make war against him that sat on the horse, and against his army.* **20** *And the beast was taken, and with him the false prophet that wrought miracles before him, with which he deceived them that had received the mark of the beast, and them that worshipped his image. These both were cast alive into a lake of fire burning with brimstone.* **21** *And the remnant were slain with the sword of him that sat upon the horse, which sword proceeded out of his mouth: and all the fowls were filled with their flesh.*

The Millennium

Step Six

MILLENNIUM MEANS 1,000. THEOLOGICALLY, THE word designates the period of time Jesus Christ rules bodily on the earth for one thousand years. After just a few years in the 3rd heaven, the Millennium is literally the Christian's first 1,000 years of heaven. Any information learned about this age helps answer the question: What is heaven like? Old Testament prophets spoke often of this dispensation. Jesus Christ rules all creation from a throne in Jerusalem.

Christ's millennial reign begins immediately following the battle of Armageddon. In other words, it begins the day Jesus Christ returns to earth. Armageddon ends quickly and in total defeat for the enemies of Christ. Revelation chapter 20 clearly depicts this 1,000 year period of time. The passage below contains information on numerous topics, but for the purposes of this study, it is used to verify the 1,000 years does indeed happen. The Millennium commencing with Jesus 2nd Advent, is an absolute biblical fact. It is not dispensational theory.

> ***Revelation 20:1-9*** *And I saw an angel come down from heaven, having the key of the bottomless pit and a great chain in his hand.* ***2*** *And he laid hold on the dragon, that old serpent, which is the Devil, and Satan,* ***and bound him a thousand years,*** ***3*** *And cast him into the bottomless pit, and shut him up, and set a seal upon him,*

*that he should deceive the nations no more, **till the thousand years should be fulfilled:** and after that he must be loosed a little season. 4 And I saw thrones, and they sat upon them, and judgment was given unto them: and I saw the souls of them that were beheaded for the witness of Jesus, and for the word of God, and which had not worshipped the beast, neither his image, neither had received his mark upon their foreheads, or in their hands; and **they lived and reigned with Christ a thousand years.** 5 But the rest of the dead lived not again **until the thousand years were finished.** This is the first resurrection. 6 Blessed and holy is he that hath part in the first resurrection: on such the second death hath no power; but they shall be priests of God and of Christ, **and shall reign with him a thousand years.** 7 And **when the thousand years are expired,** Satan shall be loosed out of his prison, 8 And shall go out to deceive the nations which are in the four quarters of the earth, Gog and Magog, to gather them together to battle: the number of whom is as the sand of the sea. 9 And they went up on the breadth of the earth, and compassed the camp of the saints about, and the beloved city: and fire came down from God out of heaven, and devoured them.*

Great White Throne

STEP SEVEN

THE GREAT WHITE THRONE JUDGMENT takes place at the end of the Millennium. Although Christians stand present, they are not being judged. Ultimately, God judged Christians at Calvary where Jesus Christ died for our sin. Jesus judged Christians for works at the Judgment seat of Christ. No Christian is judged at the Great White Throne Judgment. Christians may actually engage in helping God in this whole process. The Bible says Christians judge the world and angels. Therefore, God may even judge angels at this time.

> *1 Corinthians 6:2-3 Do ye not know that the saints shall judge the world? and if the world shall be judged by you, are ye unworthy to judge the smallest matters? 3 Know ye not that we shall judge angels? how much more things that pertain to this life?*

WHO IS JUDGED AT THE GREAT WHITE THRONE JUDGMENT?

Human beings- from Adam and Eve to the last baby born in the Millennium. All angels, (good and bad). Death's occupants, the Sea's occupants. Only the satanic trinity: Devil, Beast, False Prophet are absent. As previously discussed, God already judged the satanic trinity.

Teaching everyone judged at the Great White goes to hell is very common and very incorrect. Although God damns billions of souls at the Great White Throne, not everyone is lost. Teaching all persons go to hell ignores dispensational truth and even adds opinion to the text.

Every person who lived during the Tribulation (lost and saved) stands to be judged at the GWTJ. Every person who lived during the Millennium (lost and saved) must stand for judgment. God saves millions during the tribulation, and quite likely billions saved during the Millennium. Where will they be judged if not the Great White Throne Judgment?

Furthermore, think about an age of accountability. An infant who dies in the Church Age does not believe on the Lord Jesus Christ; therefore, the deceased infant is not a believer in the doctrinal sense. Where does the infant get judged? Where does God judge all aborted babies' souls? Where does God judge persons without the cognitive capacity to repent or believe? Wouldn't the logical place to judge these souls be at the Great White Throne?

The reason most Bible teachers conclude all persons go to hell from the GWTJ is they know works cannot save anyone. And since God judges people according to their works, many teachers conclude all people being judged must be damned. They process all humanity through doctrinal Christian truth which is, quite frankly, wrongly dividing the word of truth.

People in other eras and dispensations can become part of the family of God. Just because people are not doctrinal Christians (Bride) does not mean they go to Hell. Just think about friends of the bridegroom attending the wedding as guests, they are not the Bride, but they're still saved. Things different are not equal. One needs to be careful with logic based on partial understanding. Anyone at the Great White Throne who goes to heaven- goes due to God's righteous judgment, mercy, and grace. Ponder also, the Judgment Seat of Christ was a judgment for works; and no one went to hell from the JSC.

Revelation 20:11-15 And I saw a great white throne, and him that sat on it, from whose face the earth and the heaven fled away; and there was found no place for them. 12 And I saw the dead, small and great, stand before God; and the books were opened: and another book was opened, which is the book of life: and the dead were judged out of those things which were written in the books, according to their works. 13 And the sea gave up the dead which were in it; and death and hell delivered up the dead which were in them: and they were judged every man according to their works. 14 And death and hell were cast into the lake of fire. This is the second death. 15 And whosoever was not found written in the book of life was cast into the lake of fire.

THOUGHT TO PONDER

Notice the dead come from three separate places, **the sea, death, and hell**. Popular understanding teaches the dead go only two places, heaven or hell. But apparently physical death delivers individuals to one of four places: *Sea, Death, Hell, Heaven*

Psalms 32:2 Blessed is the man unto whom the LORD imputeth not iniquity, and in whose spirit there is no guile.

New Jerusalem

§

STEP EIGHT

IMMEDIATELY AFTER THE GREAT WHITE Throne Judgment, Jesus presents his Bride with her permanent home, New Jerusalem. Think of New Jerusalem as a 1,000 year anniversary present for the Church.

NEW JERUSALEM IS NOT THE SAME JERUSALEM THAT IS ON EARTH.

As God creates a new earth, and new heaven- he also creates New Jerusalem. New Jerusalem is like a beautiful moon, the pearl of God's Kingdom. Placed in the heaven, it orbits the earth and emanates light basking the nations below.

New Jerusalem is huge. 12,000 furlongs equals about 1,500 miles. The shape of the new, small planet remains somewhat interpretative, but it is either an inverted pyramid or cube. Since the population is finite, the size of our new home is plenty spacious.

When Christians think about Heaven, they usually think about New Jerusalem: Apostle John describes this wonderful place extensively in *Revelation 21*. The city of pure gold, the pearly gates, and the street of gold all belong to New Jerusalem. It is incorrect; however, to make New Jerusalem a synonym for heaven. New Jerusalem is only one small part of heaven. An astronomer never says earth is the universe; in the same way, a Christian needs to identify heaven correctly. Truly New Jerusalem eventually becomes a Christian's heaven, but God doesn't create the city until a thousand years after the 2ⁿᵈ Coming. Furthermore, Old Testament saints do not live in New Jerusalem; they live on earth. Ascribing heaven's real estate is a discriminating process. New Jerusalem does not have a temple

> *Revelation 21:2 And I John saw the holy city, new Jerusalem, coming down from God out of heaven, prepared as a bride adorned for her husband.*

> *Revelation 21:10-11 And he carried me away in the spirit to a great and high mountain, and shewed me that great city, the holy Jerusalem, descending out of heaven from God,* **11** *Having the glory of God: and her light was like unto a stone most precious, even like a jasper stone, clear as crystal;*

> *Revelation 21:22-26 **And I saw no temple therein:** for the Lord God Almighty and the Lamb are the temple of it.* **23** *And the city had no need of the sun, neither of the moon, to shine in it: for the glory of God did lighten it, and the Lamb is the light thereof.* **24** *And the nations of them which are saved shall walk in the light of it: and the kings of the earth do bring their glory and honour into it.* **25** *And the gates of it shall not be shut at all by day: for there shall be no night there.* **26** *And they shall bring the glory and honour of the nations into it.*

Thought to ponder:

God places his eternal temple on earth. Currently his temple exists in the sides of the north in the 3ʳᵈ heaven. But it is a different city entirely from New Jerusalem. God's throne sits in his temple on earth.

Cities Jerusalem

1. Earth's Jerusalem – presently located on earth in the Middle East.
2. Heaven's eternal Jerusalem - located in the 3rd heaven. The place of God's Throne. Also called the city on the sides of the north, and Zion. Also referred to as *the mother of us all.*
3. New Jerusalem –Immediately following the Great White Throne Judgment, God creates the new heaven, the new earth, and New Jerusalem, future home for Christians.

Scripture declares three different cities each named Jerusalem. One needs to be very discriminating, ponder carefully the evidence.

THE CITY ON THE SIDES OF THE NORTH: ETERNAL ZION JERUSALEM

Presently located in the 3rd heaven, the city holds the temple and God's throne inside the temple. Once this city is transplanted on earth, the river of life emanates from this location. And the tree of life grows along the banks of the river. The city remains God's eternal capital of the kingdom of heaven.

Psalms 48:1-2 A Song *and* Psalm for the sons of Korah. Great *is* the LORD, and greatly to be praised in the city of our God, *in* the mountain of his holiness. **2** Beautiful for situation, the joy of the whole earth, *is* mount Zion, *on* the sides of the north, the city of the great King.

The tree of life being exclusively on the earth is often contested. But opposing views largely base on the presumption that New Jerusalem- and *Jerusalem the city on the sides of the north*- are the same place. But once these cities are segregated (or rightly divided) confusion evaporates.

Revelation 22:1-5 does not describe New Jerusalem; it describes a city on the earth with God's throne inside his temple. This is the same temple presently in the 3rd heaven in the city on the sides of the north *Psalm 48:1-2*. Observe scripture declares *there will be no more curse*. New Jerusalem was never cursed, only earth was cursed. God finished describing New Jerusalem in Revelation chapter 21; that's why the chapter closed.

> *Revelation 22:1-5 And he shewed me a pure river of water of life, clear as crystal, **proceeding out of the throne of God and of the Lamb**. 2 In the midst of the street of it, and on either side of the river, was there the tree of life, which bare twelve manner of fruits, and yielded her fruit every month: and the leaves of the tree were for the healing of the nations. 3 And there shall be no more curse: but **the throne of God and of the Lamb shall be in it**; and his servants shall serve him: 4 And they shall see his face; and his name shall be in their foreheads. 5 And there shall be no night there; and they need no candle, neither light of the sun; for the Lord God giveth them light: and they shall reign for ever and ever.*

> *Ezekiel 37:26-27 Moreover I will make a covenant of peace with them; it shall be an everlasting covenant with them: and I will place them, and multiply them, and **will set my sanctuary in the midst of them for evermore**. 27 My tabernacle also shall be with them: yea, I will be their God, and they shall be my people.*

> *Psalms 46:4-5 There is a river, the streams whereof shall make glad the city of God, the holy place of the tabernacles of the most*

High. **5** *God is in the midst of her; she shall not be moved: God shall help her, and that right early.*

Ezekiel 47:1 *Afterward he brought me again unto the door of the house; and, behold, waters issued out from under the threshold of the house eastward: for the forefront of the house stood toward the east, and the waters came down from under from the right side of the house, at the south side of the altar.*

It is crucial for understanding to rightly divide the following evidence. The eternal city Jerusalem is indeed coming to earth. God's temple, wherein is His Throne, will sit on this earth. New Jerusalem, heaven for Christians, will not be on earth; nor is it the place of God's Throne.

Heaven's Headquarters

The headquarters for God's kingdom operates from Jerusalem. The capital building is a temple (made by God Himself) that houses God's throne. Notice God actually transplants geography and architecture from the 3rd heaven and places them in Israel. The passages are doctrinal/literal truths taking place during the Millennium.

Ezekiel 43:7 *And he said unto me, Son of man, **the place of my throne,** and the place of the soles of my feet, **where I will dwell in the midst of the children of Israel for ever,***

Isaiah 2:1-5 *The word that Isaiah the son of Amoz saw concerning Judah and Jerusalem. **2** And it shall come to pass in the last days, **that the mountain of the LORD'S house shall be established in the top of the mountains, and shall be exalted above the hills;** and all nations shall flow unto it. **3** And many people shall go and say, Come ye, and let us go up to the mountain of the LORD,* *to the house of the God of Jacob; and he will teach us of his ways, and we will walk in his paths: for out of Zion shall go forth the law, and the word of the LORD from Jerusalem.* **4** *And he shall judge among the nations, and shall rebuke many people: and they shall beat their swords into plowshares, and their spears into pruning-hooks: nation shall not lift up sword against nation, neither shall they learn war any more.* **5** *O house of Jacob, come ye, and let us walk in the light of the LORD.*

Ezekiel 37:26-28 Moreover I will make a covenant of peace with them; it shall be an everlasting covenant with them: and I will place them, and multiply them, **and will set my sanctuary in the midst of them for evermore.** *27 My tabernacle also shall be with them: yea, I will be their God, and they shall be my people.* **28** *And the heathen shall know that I the LORD do sanctify Israel,* **when my sanctuary shall be in the midst of them for evermore.**

These heathen are people born during the Millennium. Some of them eventually choose to serve Jesus Christ, others go to war with Jesus at the end of the 1000 years.

Summary of distinctions: **Rev. 22:1- 5 cannot be New Jerusalem for the following reasons:**

God's throne is in the temple and there is no temple in New Jerusalem. *Rev 21:22 with Rev. 22:1, 16:17, 7:15, Ezek. 43:5-7*

Rev. 22:3 implicitly states there was once a curse. New Jerusalem was never cursed. But the earth was and the earth is where heavenly Zion will be. By the time 22:3 is fulfilled, the curse is gone, and the earth will house mount Zion, the city on the sides of the north.

The river of life emanates from the temple, as it does in *Ezekiel 47:1* thus *Rev. 22:1 and Ezekiel. 47:1* describe the same place. No temple in New Jerusalem *Rev. 21:22*

Rev. 22:2 is in agreement with Ezek. *43:5-7* Again; both prophets describe the same place.

Salvation

§

IN THE JOHN CHAPTER 3, Jesus made a disturbing statement to a man named Nicodemus:

> *John 3:3 Jesus answered and said unto him, Verily, verily, I say unto thee, Except a man be born again, he cannot see the kingdom of God.*

Jesus' statement is disturbing because Nicodemus believed in God, and thought he was prepared to go to heaven, but Jesus says he was not ready. Nicodemus asks a logical question:

> *John 3:4 Nicodemus saith unto him, How can a man be born when he is old? can he enter the second time into his mother's womb, and be born?*

What exactly does Jesus mean anyway? Being *born again* is synonymous with salvation, in other words, being ready to go to heaven. The most important decision a person can make is to be born again- *Except a man be born again, he cannot see the kingdom of God.*

HAVE YOU BEEN BORN AGAIN? ARE YOU ABSOLUTELY CERTAIN YOU ARE SAVED AND WILL GO TO HEAVEN WHEN YOU DIE?

Many people are like Nicodemus. They believe in God, and they believe they are good enough (at least compared to lots of other people). Besides, with so much religious confusion, and everyone thinks they're right- what else can a person possibly do other than be good as possible?

Consider this:

Since Jesus said *you must be born again* this also means there was a time in your life when you were not born again. Do you remember a time when you were not saved?

Compare this question to asking a married couple when they got married. A married person may forget the day or the year of the wedding, but it is very unlikely anyone forgets being single. In other words, they remember when they were not married. Lots of people forget the exact date of their anniversary, but no one forgets the wedding happened.

Do you remember when you were not saved?
If you can't remember being lost, you are probably not saved.

Imagine standing before God on Judgment Day, and God asks, **What have you done to deserve heaven?** What is your answer? Below is a sampling of wrong answers:

- I believe in God
- Basically I'm a good person.
- Although I'm a sinner, I did my best.
- I am generous with my money.
- I help people whenever I can.
- I'm not that bad, compared to some.
- I go to church.
- I pray.
- I have been baptized.
- I have been confirmed.

These answers are all wrong because they imply a person must earn heaven by good works. Most people believe they go to heaven because they are good enough. They conclude a loving God lets them in to heaven because they are basically OK. But this conclusion also rejects one's personal need for a Saviour.

* What do you believe?
* Are you counting on good works or Jesus?
* Do you want to get just what you deserve?

Personal moral goodness does not earn salvation. One can be religiously and morally good and still reject Jesus Christ. Actually, this is the difference between Christianity and all other religions. After all is said and done, every other religion (including secular humanism) teaches the way people behave (moral conduct) earns their eternal reward. While Christianity teaches the only way to heaven is by making Jesus Christ your personal Saviour. Through faith, God covers your sin with His blood, and gives you the righteousness of Jesus Christ. Salvation is a gift; accepting that gift by faith is the only thing a person can do.

The verses below reveal God's conclusion on the moral goodness of mankind. As you can see, any bragging about personal goodness is pride and foolishness.

Romans 3:10-18 As it is written, There is none righteous, no, not one: 11 There is none that understandeth, there is none that seeketh after God. 12 They are all gone out of the way, they are together become unprofitable; there is none that doeth good, no, not one. 13 Their throat is an open sepulchre; with their tongues they have used deceit; the poison of asps is under their lips: 14 Whose mouth is full of cursing and bitterness: 15 Their feet are swift to shed blood: 16 Destruction and misery are in their ways: 17 And the way of peace have they not known: 18 There is no fear of God before their eyes.

According to God's Word, we are all sinners and in need of repentance. Don't deceive yourself because so many people are worse than you. Repentance means being willing to change or turn from old attitudes, and ideas about God, just as much as it means being willing to change behavior. It may be your life style isn't all that bad, but have you been saved?

Going to church, giving money to worthy causes, and moral goodness is commendable, but beware; you can be a good person and still be lost. When it comes to getting into heaven, the only righteousness God accepts is the righteousness of Jesus Christ. And the only way to get Christ's righteousness is to believe in Him and ask Jesus to save you. When a person makes Jesus his/her Saviour, Jesus imputes or gives His righteousness to them.

Romans 3:21-25 But now the righteousness of God without the law is manifested, being witnessed by the law and the prophets; 22 Even the righteousness of God which is by faith of Jesus Christ unto all and upon all them that believe: for there is no difference: 23 For all have sinned, and come short of the glory of God; 24 Being justified freely by his grace through the redemption that is in Christ Jesus: 25 Whom God hath set forth to be a propitiation through faith in his blood, to declare his righteousness for the remission of sins that are past, through the forbearance of God;

Ephesians 2:8-9 For by grace are ye saved through faith; and that not of yourselves: it is the gift of God: 9 Not of works, lest any man should boast.

John 3:16 For God so loved the world, that he gave his only begotten Son, that whosoever believeth in him should not perish, but have everlasting life.

Romans 10:9-10 *That if thou shalt confess with thy mouth the Lord Jesus, and shalt believe in thine heart that God hath raised him from the dead, thou shalt be saved.* **10** *For with the heart man believeth unto righteousness; and with the mouth confession is made unto salvation.*

Romans 10:13 *For whosoever shall call upon the name of the Lord shall be saved.*

In our natural condition we are separated from God by our sin. The whole world is a morally fallen mess. No one is born righteous, good, or in love with God. There comes a time in your life when you must make a choice. And the choice is to get saved or to stay lost.

Have you ever acknowledged your own lost condition and your need of salvation? A person can actually believe the Bible and still be trusting in his/her own good works. A lot of church going folks never call on the Lord for their own personal salvation. Do you remember a time in your life when you prayed for the Lord Jesus Christ to save you? If your answer is no, or you are not sure, read the verses below and do it now.

Romans 10:13 *For whosoever shall call upon the name of the Lord shall be saved.*

There is no other way. No other religion. No other God. Jesus, alone, is the Saviour of your soul. Salvation is in Christ alone. Without Jesus Christ as your Saviour you are lost. The Bible is very plain.

John 14:6 *Jesus saith unto him, I am the way, the truth, and the life: no man cometh unto the Father, but by me.*

John 14:9 *Jesus saith unto him, Have I been so long time with you, and yet hast thou not known me, Philip? he that hath seen* *me hath seen the Father; and how sayest thou then, Shew us the Father?*

1 John 5:12-13 *He that hath the Son hath life; and he that hath not the Son of God hath not life. **13** These things have I written unto you that believe on the name of the Son of God; that ye may know that ye have eternal life, and that ye may believe on the name of the Son of God.*

John 3:15-17 *That whosoever believeth in him should not perish, but have eternal life. 16 For God so loved the world, that he gave his only begotten Son, that whosoever believeth in him should not perish, but have everlasting life. 17 For God sent not his Son into the world to condemn the world; but that the world through him might be saved.*

Romans 10:9-13 *That if thou shalt confess with thy mouth the Lord Jesus, and shalt believe in thine heart that God hath raised him from the dead, thou shalt be saved. **10** For with the heart man believeth unto righteousness; and with the mouth confession is made unto salvation. **11** For the scripture saith, Whosoever believeth on him shall not be ashamed. **12** For there is no difference between the Jew and the Greek: for the same Lord over all is rich unto all that call upon him. **13** For whosoever shall call upon the name of the Lord shall be saved.*

End

Books written by Joseph Dulmage

Angels, Giants, and Things under the Earth
Approaching Adventure; Understanding Heaven
Distress of Souls; Yet Trouble Came
Divorce and Remarriage, For Christians
GAP
Healing
Leviathan's Nightmare
Serious and Unusual Christian Fiction
Tongues
What Might This Parable Be?

About the Author

§

JOSEPH DULMAGE WAS BORN IN 1955 in Detroit, Michigan. He graduated from Eastern Michigan University with a degree in secondary educa-tion with an emphasis in his-tory, psychology, and social studies. Dulmage worked as a chaplain in the federal prison Life Connections Program.

He served as the facili-tator in FCI Milan and has worked in several federal prisons, including USP Leavenworth, USP Terre Haute, and Petersburg, Virginia. He also served as the director of prisoner aftercare for the national office of Volunteers of America.

He has been a public school teacher, Bible teacher, counselor, freelance writer, and contributing writer for Truthought Corrective Thinking LLC.

Made in the USA
Monee, IL
24 July 2021